Celebrating your year

1967

a very special year for

_____

_____

_____

_____

_____

A message from the author:

Welcome to the year 1967.

I trust you will enjoy this fascinating romp down memory lane.

And when you have reached the end of the book, please join me in the battle against AI generated copy-cat books and fake reviews.

Details are at the back of the book.*

Best regards,
Bernard Bradforsand-Tyler.

Contents

1967 Family Life in the USA	9
Life in the United Kingdom	13
Our Love Affair with Cars	19
Television's Race to Color	25
Most Popular TV Shows of 1967	26
The Cold War–Nuclear Arms Race	29
The Cold War–Space Race	30
The Cold War–Battlefield Vietnam	34
Anti-Vietnam Protests	35
The Long, Hot Summer of Riots	36
China's Cultural Revolution	40
The Six-Day War in the Middle East	41
1967 in Cinema and Film	44
Top Grossing Films of the Year	45
Espionage Films of 1967	47
Musical Memories	49
San Francisco's Summer of Love	50
Wes Wilson's Psychedelic Concert Posters	53
1967 Billboard Top 30 Songs	54
Fashion Trends of the 1960s	57
Science and Technology	65
Also in Sports	67
Other News from 1967	68
Famous People Born in 1967	72
1967 in Numbers	76
Image Attributions	84

Advertisement

Total Electric Living is a clean break with the past

The flameless electric clothes dryer is America's No. 1 choice for permanent-press fabrics

The makers of permanent-press garments recommend *tumble drying* as the best way to keep creases sharp and textures soft. And this, among other reasons, is why American women prefer the flameless electric clothes dryer. It's their first choice by far.

Gentle electric heat "relaxes" synthetic fabrics for proper wrinkle-resistance. Clothes come out soft, fresh-looking, ready to wear.

A flameless electric dryer has many more advantages. It's marvelously clean. Costs less to buy. And it doesn't require a special flue, which enables you to install it anywhere you choose.

So why dry outdoors? Why fight rain, dust, soot and cold? Make a clean break with the past. See your appliance dealer about a flameless electric dryer... another appliance that adds to the joy of Total Electric Living.

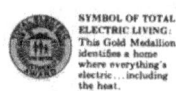

SYMBOL OF TOTAL ELECTRIC LIVING: This Gold Medallion identifies a home where everything's electric... including the heat.

You Live Better Electrically
Edison Electric Institute, 750 Third Avenue, New York, N.Y. 10017.

The flameless electric clothes dryer is America's No.1 choice for permanent-press fabrics

The makers of permanent-press garments recommend *tumble drying* as the best way to keep creases sharp and textures soft. And this, among other reasons, is why American women prefer the flameless electric clothes dryer. It's their first choice by far.

Gentle electric heat "relaxes" synthetic fabrics for proper wrinkle-resistance. Clothes come out soft, fresh-looking, ready to wear.

A flameless electric dryer has many more advantages. It's marvelously clean. Costs less to buy. And it doesn't require a special flue, which enables you to install it anywhere you choose.

So why dry outdoors? Why fight rain, dust, soot and cold? Make a clean break with the past. See your appliance dealer about a flameless electric dryer... another appliance that adds to the joy of Total Electric Living

You live better electrically

Let's flashback to 1967, a very special year.

Was this the year you were born?

Was this the year you were married?

Whatever the reason, this book is a celebration of your year,

THE YEAR 1967.

Turn the pages to discover a book packed with fun-filled fabulous facts. We look at the people, the places, the politics and the pleasures that made 1967 unique and helped shape the world we know today.

So get your time-travel suit on, and enjoy this trip down memory lane, to rediscover what life was like, back in the year 1967.

Advertisement

Less Lens, $195.50
but you need a lens, of course, maybe two, maybe more...

That's the point! Only Mamiya twin-lens reflexes let you make such a choice. There are five lenses from 65mm wide angle to 180mm telephoto. And they're interchangeable.

Gives you quite an advantage. No matter what the problem: image size, picture angle, perspective, you know you've got the situation well in hand.

The Mamiya C33, shown here, is the *automatic* model with shutter-cocking film crank (no accidental double exposures). It also has an automatic parallax compensator, an automatic closeup exposure-factor indicator, expanded distance scales, and a host of other features.

The C22 (not shown) is the *standard* model without crank and without some of the other special C33 features, but with the same sturdy construction and picture-taking qualities. Also costs $65.60 less.

All lenses and accessories can be used with both models. See them at your dealer, or write. Mamiya division of Ehrenreich Photo-Optical Industries, Inc., Garden City, N.Y.

Family Life in 1967 America

Imagine if time-travel was a reality, and one fine morning you wake up to find yourself flashed back in time, back to the year 1967.

What would life be like for a typical family, in a typical town, somewhere in America?

A typical middle-class young family relaxing at home in 1967.

The 1960s was a decade of change, of shifting social movements, of vibrant and vocal youth, of rebellion and rejection. Yet, what we fondly refer to as "The Sixties", really only began in the middle of the decade. The first half of the decade more rightly belonged to the Post-War era, the era of the Baby Boomers (1946-1964).

By the mid-'60s, the first of the Baby Boomers were making themselves heard. Their views, aspirations and demands would shape America, and the world, for decades to come. In 1967, conservative America would be rocked by a new uprising—as the hippies of San Francisco radiated across the nation and exploded into our consciousness.

It began in the hippie enclave of San Francisco's Haight-Ashbury, where musicians and creatives had been developing a new way of living. Their social experiment challenged the status quo, welcoming freedom of expression for everything from fashion, music and literature, to communal living, hallucinogenic drug use, and free love.

On 14th January, a crowd of 30,000 gathered at Golden Gate Park for an event known as the *Human Be-In*, to "turn on, tune in, drop out".[1]

The media coverage spurred youth across the country to join in the movement, culminating in what would become known as the "Summer of Love". As many as 100,000 college and high-school students headed to Haight-Ashbury in their spring break, overwhelming the residents with overcrowding, homelessness, hunger, crime and trash. Similar events formed elsewhere in California, Denver and New York, spreading the hippie experiment across the nation and throughout the western world.

Above: Poster for the first Human Be-In.

Below: Attendees at Golden Gate Park.

During the '60s, we benefited from America's longest ever period of continuous economic growth, averaging 5% GDP growth annually.

We were more likely to be working in offices, rather than tilling the land or working on assembly lines. We had more spending power than ever before. And we enjoyed an excessive consume-and-discard culture, driven by a mature advertising industry which instilled in us the belief that we constantly needed more and more, bigger and better.

But beyond the excessive consumerism and pleasure-filled amusements, we were also fighting for a better world. Students rallied against the draft, feminists demanded gender equality, African Americans marched for civil rights, professors held teach-ins, and everywhere, our citizens were standing up against US involvement in the Vietnam War.

1967 was not just *The Summer of Love*, the year is also remembered by another moniker: *The Long, Hot Summer of Riots*.

Top: Anti-war protest in Harlem, 1967.
Above: Pittsburgh Veterans for Peace protest on Memorial Bridge, Washington, DC. Oct 1967.

Average costs in 1967 [1]	
New house	$20,994
New car	$2,750
Refrigerator	$300
Washing Machine	$200
A gallon of gasoline	$0.32

The median household income was $7,200 a year.[2] Unemployment stood at 3.8%, with GDP growth at 2.7%.[3]

[1] thepeoplehistory.com and mclib.info/reference/local-history-genealogy/historic-prices/.
[2] census.gov/library/publications/1968/demo/p60-57.html.
[3] thebalance.com/unemployment-rate-by-year-3305506.

Advertisement

Only new 1967 Admiral Duplex comes in 4 sizes, has the 5 features women want most!

No-frost Admiral Duplex Freezer/Refrigerator offers you even bigger capacities and more exclusive features, still fits your kitchen space!

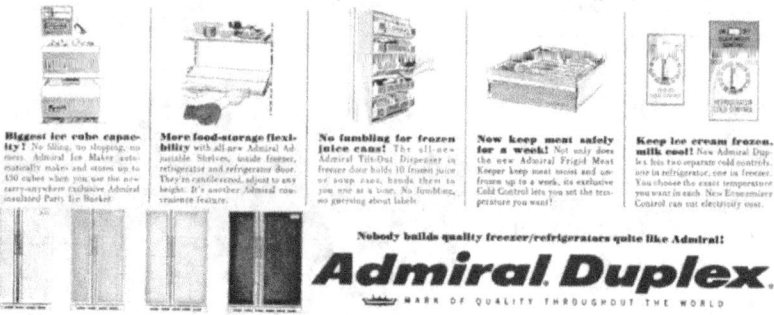

Nobody builds quality freezer/refrigerators quite like Admiral!

Admiral Duplex.
MARK OF QUALITY THROUGHOUT THE WORLD

Only new 1967 Admiral Duplex comes in 4 sizes, has the 5 features women want most!

Biggest ice cube capacity! No filling, no slopping, no mess. Admiral Ice Make automatically makes and stores up to 430 cubes when you use the new carry-anywhere exclusive Admiral insulated Party Ice Bucket.

More food-storage flexibility with all-new Admiral Adjustable Shelves, inside freezer, refrigerator and refrigerator door. They're cantilevered, adjust to any height. It's another Admiral convenience feature.

No fumbling for frozen juice cans! The all-new Admiral Tilt-Out Dispenser in freezer door holds 10 frozen juice or soup cans, hands them to you one at a time. No fumbling, no guessing about labels.

Now keep meat safely for a week! Not only does the new Admiral Frigid Meat keeper keep meat moist and unfrozen up to a week, its exclusive Cold Control lets you set the temperature you want!

Keep ice cream frozen, milk cool! New Admiral Duplex has two separate cold controls, one in refrigerator, one in freezer. You choose the exact temperature you want in each. New Economizer Control can cut electricity cost.

Nobody builds quality freezer/refrigerators quite like Admiral!
Admiral Duplex. Mark of quality throughout the world.

Life in the United Kingdom

Now just imagine you flashed back to a town in 1967 England or Western Europe.

London's "Swinging Sixties" was now center stage for music, arts, fashion, and all things cultural.

With the ravages of war firmly in the past, the cultural revolution known as the Swinging Sixties quickly became the United Kingdom's greatest export of the decade. Focused on fun-loving hedonism and rejection of traditional conservatism, this was a revolution full of excitement, freedom and hope. Unlike their American counterparts, UK's Baby Boomers were free of conscription and the miseries of war.

Turning heads in the latest "Dolly Bird" fashions on Carnaby Street, London, 1967.

From the mid to late '60s, artists, musicians, writers, designers, film-makers, photographers, and all types of creatives and intellectuals descended on London. Their radical views brought about a revolution in social and sexual politics.

Musicians led the charge with their own uniquely British sound. Influenced by rock 'n' roll of the '50s, yet infused with innovative new rhythms and sounds, their songs inspired their fans to express individuality and freedom.

The Who, 1966.

The Beatles.

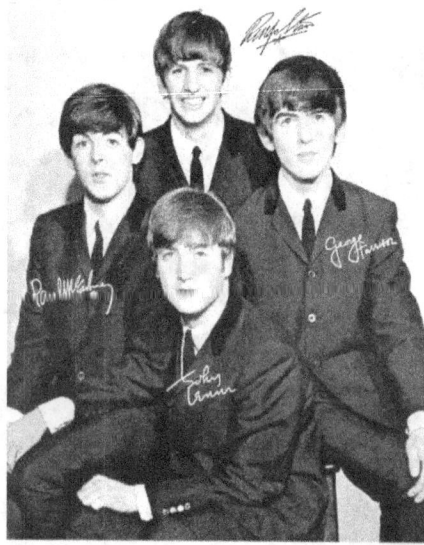

The Rolling Stones, 1966.

Pirate radio stations brought "the London Sound" to the airwaves, pushing bands like The Rolling Stones, The Kinks, The Yardbirds, and The Who, along with early '60s mega-band The Beatles.

In fashion, designer Mary Quant created youthful styles for running, jumping and dancing in. Along with other trend-setting designers, the fashion scene centered around London's Carnaby Street and King's Road in Kensington.

London also introduced us to the first non-aristocratic looking supermodels, who soon became household names. Through magazines worldwide, they guided us on the newest trends in urban style and street wear.

'60s supermodels Jean Shrimpton and Twiggy.

In literature, retired British spy Jean Le Carré penned unstoppable mystery thrillers infused with cold-war espionage. He, along with crowd-pleasing British favorites like Agatha Christie, Alistair MacLean, and Victor Canning, became instant International best sellers.

British film-makers captured the high-spirited fun and sexual freedom of Swinging London with experimental, mischievous comedies focused on themes of escape and young, free love.

Advertisement

University tests prove an Automatic Royal can help your youngster do better in school.

Tests conducted at Boston University, Columbia, and the University of Illinois prove that using a typewriter improves a youngster's word skills, stimulates creativity and has a "generally favorable effect on academic achievement."

And Royals give students more of these educational values because Royals are more automatic–do more of the typing job automatically. A Royal lets your student better concentrate on his schoolwork instead of his typing. Schoolwork improves because:

A Royal is a great organizer... of thoughts, term papers, and teenagers. Somehow, when a youngster begins to type his work, he catches errors and thinks better. His work improves. He writes longer, fuller reports.

A Royal improves reading comprehension... the crisp, black and white print of a Royal is easier to read than longhand (for teacher, too!)

A Royal makes homework almost fun... to a teenager, a new Royal is a tool, a status symbol, and a fun thing all rolled into one. So he wants to spend extra time with it. (And he ends up by spending more time on his homework.)

The new all-electric Ultronic is the most automatic Royal... with an electric carriage return that moves at the touch of a key. (Takes over 97% of the work of typing!)

Look and see how automatic the Royal manual portables are, too. Take the Safari with exclusive Magic Margin... or the smart Parade with so many office-typewriter features... or the compact, rugged Royalite. From $49.95.

Swinging London was largely seen as a middle-class consumer-driven diversion, centered around the fashionable West End. Elsewhere, counter sub-cultures existed, such as the Mods and the Rockers. The groups were easily identified by their outfits and choice of vehicles, the Rockers on their motorbikes wore leather jackets, while the Mods on their mirror-decked scooters preferred Italian-cut suits.

In the mid-'60s violent clashes between the Rockers and Mods erupted, leaving both groups branded as trouble-makers.

Throughout the decade, British families gained greater purchasing power and disposable incomes. Stable economic growth led to rising living standards with excess cash to spend on leisure and amusements.

Home ownership rose markedly as a 20-year post-war construction boom provided much needed affordable housing stock. A "job for life" was a reality, and job security made home ownership widely attainable.

Education for girls, and the growth of feminism, saw more young women entering the workforce. Although equality was still a long way off, it was now possible to be female, single, living away from home, and independent.

Advertisement

If you've settled for anything less than a Pontiac, turn the page. Quick.

If you've settled for anything less than a Pontiac, turn the page. Quick.

Too late. Now we're going to tell you that a luxurious Pontiac Catalina actually sells for the same money as many models of the low-priced three.

And that it comes with a powerful new 400 cubic inch V-8 (standard). And a big-car 121-inch wheelbase (standard). And such things as our exclusive disappearing windshield wipers, a padded instrument panel with wood grain styling, full nylon blend carpeting and some very posh interiors of rich, long-wearing Morrokide (standard). Plus a host of new safety features like passenger-guard door locks, a four-way hazard warning flasher and a dual master cylinder brake system (all standard).

You say you really hadn't decided yet, but that now you're headed for your nearest Pontiac dealer? Shrewd move.

Wide-Track Pontiac

Our Love Affair with Cars

Our love affair with cars began way back in the early '50s, and by 1967 we were irreversibly addicted to our vehicles. Vehicle numbers continued to rise year-on-year as the cost of a standard family car became increasingly more affordable. Although car costs had risen markedly, so too had real wages.

Increased car ownership and the creation of the National Highway System gave Americans a new sense of freedom. Office commuters could live further out from the crowded and decaying city centers, and commute quickly and comfortably to work.

Rush hour traffic, New York in the mid-'60s.

Rural areas were no longer isolated, benefiting from access to food, medical and other supplies. The suburbanization of America, which had begun a decade earlier, now saw nearly half the population living in the suburbs. The car was no longer a luxury, it was a necessity.

Northland Mall carpark in the mid-'60s, Columbus, Ohio.

Catering to the suburban lifestyle, fully enclosed, air-conditioned shopping malls sprang up country-wide during the 1960s. A typical mall design saw one or two anchor stores surrounded by hundreds of smaller specialty shops, sitting within a vast expanse of carparks.

Advertisement

Introducing The White Hots!

They glitter, they gleam, they're the fabulous collection of White Hot '67 Fords now at your Ford dealer's.

Specially built, equipped, and priced to move–fast!

White Hot Ford Galaxie 500 2-door hardtops, with all these extras: special wheel covers, whitewalls, accent stripes, plus your choice of 6 two-tone paint jobs.

White Hot Ford Custom 500 sedans, 2- or 4-door, white or blue, with extras like special trim, whitewalls, XL wheel covers. Come see them all today!

(Comparison shoppers welcome.)

Ford Dealers' 4th Annual White Sale.

Detroit was America's car manufacturing powerhouse, where "the Big Three" (Ford, General Motors and Chrysler) produced 90% of cars sold in the country. Using technological innovation, with significant financial and marketing strength, the Big Three successfully bought out or edged out all smaller competitors throughout the '50s and '60s.

Big cars ruled the roads during the "Golden Age of Muscle Cars" (1964-1970). These high-performance coupes usually came with large, powerful V-8 engines and rear wheel drive. Also known as "super cars" they were designed with drag-racing engine capability to satisfy our desire for power above all else.

1967 Chrysler 300 Convertible.

By 1967 there were 80 million vehicles on US roads. Car sales were at all-time highs, as were motor vehicle fatalities. 50,724 car-related deaths were recorded during the year, the result of dangerous driving and unsafe vehicles.[1]

1967 Cadillac Convertible by GM.

Led in part by the success of the imported Volkswagen Beetle and the growing counter-culture movement, consumer demand began shifting towards smaller, more compact, cheaper and safer vehicles. The scene was set for Japanese small car manufacturers to take on the Big Three.

[1] en.wikipedia.org/wiki/Motor_vehicle_fatality_rate_in_U.S._by_year.

Five car-producing countries dominated the industry in the first half of the decade: England, France, Germany and Italy, with America in top spot. However, Japan stormed into this elite group with a swift and dramatic expansion of its automobile industry. By 1967 Japan would position itself in second place, behind only America, for total number of vehicles produced.

Japanese domestic demand had grown rapidly in the early '60s through sales of ultra-compact and affordable *kei cars*. Mass production of mid-sized family cars, more suited to international export, soon followed.

1967 Toyota Corona.

Japanese cars were safer to drive, reliable, affordable, compact, efficient and popular, quickly making Toyota, Nissan, Mitsubishi, Mazda and Honda the export market leaders.

1967 Datsun 1300 Sedan.

1967 Honda N360.

With automobile exports increasing nearly 200% during the '60s, the Japanese car industry was well on its way to world domination.

Advertisement

"Revolt against kiddy car compacts. Go '67 Dart!"

How about you? Still smouldering about the size and shape of today's compact cars? You know the kind. Alarmingly small on the inside... amazingly dull on the outside. Cool it. There's a new way to go. Big-new, all-new Dodge Dart GT for 1967. And if its obvious beauty and fresh styling don't turn you on, maybe this list of standard equipment will. An all-vinyl interior. Bucket seats. Carpeting, front and rear. Retractable front lap belts. Redesigned, recessed instrument panel. Curved side glass. Unique, concave rear window. And more... much more luxury than you'd expect from a car carrying a compact price. Add to this a choice of Six or V8 power and a dozen or more safety features, and you've got quite a car. So, stop toying with the notion that a compact has to be dull, boxy and uninspired. Sign up for a bold, new '67 Dart GT. Pleasant duty, we assure you. The Dodge Rebellion wants you.

'67 Dodge Dart

Advertisement

New snap-on "Sun-Shield" TV!

Model PN1319

New Admiral 16" "Sun-Shield" TV with Instant Play, PNC7827.

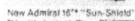

New Admiral 19" "Instant Play" TV with roll-about stand, PNC9027.

Now Admiral "Instant Play" Portable gives you perfect pictures outdoors, too! Want to watch TV outdoors, in sunshine? Just snap the special black-glass sun-filter screen on this new Admiral "Sun-Shield" TV.

Unlike ordinary TV pictures that "fade out" in bright light, Admiral "Sun-Shield" portables let you enjoy sharp, clear black-and-white pictures even in brightest sunlight! Snap the screen off, enjoy perfect pictures indoors, too.

And new Admiral "Sun-Shield" TV also gives you Instant Play... just turn it on, picture and sound are there immediately... no waiting for warm-up. See it, in action, at your Admiral Dealer's now. It's available in two popular screen sizes. New Admiral "Sun-Shield" TV, the portable that brings its own shade!

Admiral
MARK OF QUALITY THROUGHOUT THE WORLD

*Screen sizes picture meas. diag.: 15", 76 sq. in.; 16", 149 sq. in.; 19", 172 sq. in. Admiral, Chicago. Admiral Canada, Ontario.

New snap-on "Sun-Shield" TV

Now Admiral "Instant Play" Portable gives you perfect pictures outdoors, too! Want to watch TV outdoors, in sunshine? Just snap the special black-glass sun-filter screen on this new Admiral "Sun-Shield" TV.

Unlike ordinary TV pictures that "fade out" in bright light, Admiral "Sun-Shield" portables let you enjoy sharp, clear black-and-white pictures even in brightest sunlight! Snap the screen off, enjoy perfect pictures indoors, too.

And new Admiral "Sun-Shield" TV also gives you Instant Play... just turn it on, picture and sound are there immediately... no waiting for warm-up. See it, in action, at your Admiral Dealer's now. It's available in two popular screen sizes. New Admiral "Sun-Shield" TV, the portable that brings its own shade!

Television's Race to Color

Those of us old enough will remember when black and white television was the norm. We neither questioned it nor demanded anything different. Although color televisions had been around since the early '50s, color broadcasts did not become commonplace in America till 1966. By 1967, the three major networks aired their entire primetime programs in color. There remained one minor problem however–most households did not own a color TV set.

By 1967, 93% of American households owned a television set (84% in the UK)[1], of which around only 15% were color sets. By 1971 that figure would jump to nearly 50%.[2]

Family TV time in the mid-'60s.

1967 was the year the UK commenced color TV broadcasts. Canada had begun one year earlier. Elsewhere, access to color TV lagged far behind. Australia only received their first color broadcasts in 1975.

Outside the USA, the television networks of many countries, were government owned or subsidized. This allowed for more focus on serious documentaries and news broadcasts, without the constant concern of generating advertising revenue.

[1] americancentury.omeka.wlu.edu/items/show/136.
[2] tvobscurities.com/articles/color60s/.

Most Popular TV Shows of 1967

1	The Andy Griffith Show	11	Bewitched
2	The Lucy Show	12	The Beverly Hillbillies
3	Gomer Pyle, U.S.M.C.	13	The Ed Sullivan Show
4	Gunsmoke	14	The Virginian
=	Family Affair	15	Friday Night Movies
=	Bonanza	=	Green Acres
7	The Red Skelton Show	17	The Lawrence Welk Show
8	The Dean Martin Show	18	The Smothers Brothers Comedy Hour
9	The Jackie Gleason Show	19	Gentle Ben
10	Saturday Night at the Movies	20	Tuesday Night at the Movies

* From the Nielsen Media Research 1967-'68 season of top-rated primetime television series in the USA.

Musical variety shows remained ever popular in 1967, with westerns and dramas added to the mix. But sitcoms continued to pull the highest ratings, with four of the top five programs of 1967 being situation comedies.

Above: Jim Nabors and Frank Sutton in *Gomer Pyle, U.S.M.C.* (CBS. 1964-1969).

Left: Lucille Ball and Vivian Vance in *The Lucy Show* (CBS. 1962-1968).

Below: Elizabeth Montgomery, Dick York and Agnes Moorehead in *Bewitched* (ABC. 1964-1972).

The Lucy Show was Lucille Ball's follow-up to the hugely successful *I Love Lucy*. Ball would win Emmy Awards for the '67 and '68 seasons.

The sitcom fantasy *Bewitched* aired for eight seasons in the '60s and continues to air today as international reruns.

Carol Burnett in *The Carol Burnett Show* (CBS. 1967-1978).

Frank Converse and Jack Warden in *N.Y.P.D.* (ABC. 1967-1969).

The television networks were quick to turn out new programs to keep us tuning in. Here are just a few of the new programs that aired for the first time in 1967: *The Carol Burnett Show, The Flying Nun, N.Y.P.D., Love Is a Many Splendored Thing, Ironside* (1967-'78), *The Phil Donahue Show* (1967-'96), and *Spiderman* (original animated series).

Raymond Burr as Robert T. Ironside with Victoria Shaw in *Ironside* (NBC. 1967-1975).

Donahue (right) with guest Johnny Carson on *The Phil Donahue Show* (NBC. 1967-1974).

Advertisement

Swanson frozen 3 course dinners

Everything from Soup to Dessert, Swanson frozen 3 course dinners

Leave it to Swanson to give you a complete Turkey Dinner like this. Just look at all the good things you get.

Start with Campbell's famous Cream of Tomato Soup. Smooth. Savory.

Then, the main course: tender turkey, good brown gravy, and Pepperidge Farm dressing. Green peas in butter sauce for extra flavor. Whole potatoes whipped in mild and creamery butter.

The sweet part: Apple crisp. A dish of spiced-up apples with a crispy, crunchy topping. A complete dinner with everything from soup to dessert.

Enjoy all five 3 Course Dinners: Turkey, Salisbury Steak, Beef, Fried Chicken, and new Mixed Seafood Grill.

Swanson frozen 3 course dinners

The Cold War–Nuclear Arms Race

Cold War tensions between the two former allies–the USSR and the USA–dominated our lives throughout the '50s and '60s. Starting in the USA as policies for communist containment, the distrust and misunderstanding between the two sides quickly escalated from political squabbling to a military nuclear arms race. And for more than 40 years, the Nuclear Arms Race gave the two superpowers the pretext needed to test nuclear bombs on a massive scale.

During the 1960s, America's global nuclear stockpiles increased rapidly, peaking in 1967 with 31,255 nuclear weapons, against the Soviet's 8,339 weapons. Joining the superpowers in this elite group were–the UK (380 weapons), France (36 weapons), and China (25 weapons) and newcomer Israel (2 weapons).[1]

The 1960s also saw a rapid escalation in nuclear weapons testing. These tests served to understand the effectiveness and capacity of each bomb type, and to act as a deterrent to enemy nations. In 1967, the US carried out 42 nuclear tests, mostly at the Nevada Proving Grounds, while USSR tested 17 nuclear bombs. Although most of the test sites were largely uninhabited by humans, some of them were densely populated. The effects of radioactive fallout plagued local populations for years afterwards.

10th Oct– US & USSR signed a treaty to ban nuclear weapons testing in outer space.

Top: China's first hydrogen bomb test, 17th June 1967.

Right: Bomb test at the Nevada Proving Grounds, circa 1960s.

[1] tandfonline.com/doi/pdf/10.2968/066004008.

The Cold War–Space Race

Throughout the 1960s, the Cold War dominated our lives on the ground and in the skies. Cold War tensions affected everything from our politics and education, to our interests in fashion and popular culture. During this time, the USSR achieved many firsts, putting them at a military, technological and intellectual advantage.

Sputnik 1 was the world's first artificial earth satellite, launched in 1957. Yuri Gagarin became the first human to orbit the earth in 1961, while Valentina Tereshkova became the first woman in space in 1963. In 1965, Alexei Leonov became the first human to walk in space.

Yuri Gagarin, first man in space.

Valentina Tereshkova, first woman in space.

Alexei Leonov, first person to walk in space.

The USSR continued to take the lead with longer space flights, space walks, and other complex maneuvers. In October 1967, two unmanned spacecraft launched into low earth orbit. Kosmos 186 and Kosmos 188 carried out the first fully automated space docking. After 3.5 hours of joint flight the two craft separated and continued their orbits.

The US continued its spending on education and defense in a bid to catch up with the Soviets. NASA had been established in 1958, and in 1961, US President John F. Kennedy declared that America would land a man on the moon. The moon had become the ultimate Space Race goal.

By 1967, NASA was ready to launch the first of its crewed Apollo missions, with the goal of setting man on the moon. Apollo 1 was to be a low orbital test of the Apollo command and service module.

On 27th Jan, tragedy struck on the launch pad at Cape Kennedy during a pre-flight rehearsal. Fire ripped through the command module while astronauts Virgil Grissom, Edward White and Roger Chaffee were seated within. Unable to operate the hatch release in time, the astronauts died of carbon monoxide asphyxia with severe burns.

Apollo 1 crew; Grissom, White and Chaffee.

Exterior of Apollo 1 after the fire.

Future crewed Apollo missions were delayed while NASA investigated the accident. The USA would achieve its goal, winning the space race in 1969, when Apollo 11 landed on the moon. Astronauts Neil Armstrong and Edwin "Buzz" Aldrin walked on the surface of the moon for $2\tfrac{1}{4}$ hours.

Buzz Aldrin walks on the moon. Photo by Neil Armstrong, 20th July 1969.

Advertisement

Can a Siegler gas heater find love and happiness in a modern living room?

Can a Siegler gas heater find love and happiness in a modern living room?

When it's tall, dark and handsome like this Mark III Georgetown model, it can. Never before has a heating unit been so attractive. The rich cherrywood vinyl-clad steel cabinet can be placed anywhere, den or dining room. And yet beneath it all is a hard-working gas heater. Front and side vents flood comfortable heat to every room while a complete circulation cycle keeps the air fresh at all times. Gas is the economical way to heat your home. It's clean, quiet, and dependable, too. The Mark III Georgetown is only one of a wide variety of famous Siegler units. If you want the best for heating your home or business, insist on Siegler. And because it's gas, you'll love it even more. See your dealer or gas company or write to: Siegler Heater Div., Lear Siegler, Inc. Brooks Drive, Centralia, Ill. 62801; Gas makes the difference. Costs less, too.

American Gas Association, Inc.

Advertisement

Do your taxes the easy way!

Add, subtract, multiply ...electrically!

Less than $90.

This year breeze through your trying tax problems with super-accurate speed. Do all your figuring with a flick of the finger.

Compare the Smith-Corona® Figurematic® with any other machine that can add, subtract, multiply and total up to 999,999.99...electrically.

For the price, you can't beat it.

FULLY PORTABLE. The Figurematic is ideal for home or office. So stylish it fits in anywhere. And travels in its own streamlined snap-on case — with retractable carrying handle. Weighs a mere 8 lbs.

FIVE-YEAR GUARANTEE. The new Figurematic now carries the same generous parts warranty* as do all Smith-Corona portable typewriters and adding machines.

TRY IT AT YOUR DEALERS NOW. Any office-equipment dealer or department store will be glad to demonstrate exactly what this low-cost, all-electric adding machine can do. Tax computation. Inventories. Purchase totals. Budgets. Statistical analysis. Even school work.

You may even forget how to add, subtract and multiply. But we figure you've got better things to do with your time anyway.

the new Smith-Corona Figurematic
MADE IN AMERICA
SCM CORPORATION 410 Park Avenue, New York, N.Y. 10022
Offices in Canada and major cities throughout the world

Do your taxes the easy way! Add, subtract, multiply... electrically! Less than $90.

This year breeze through your trying tax problems with super-accurate speed. Do all your figuring with a flick of the finger.

Compare the Smith-Corona Figurematic with any other machine that can add, subtract, multiply and total up to 999,999.99... electrically.

For the price, you can't beat it.

Fully portable. The Figurematic is ideal for home or office. So stylish it fits in anywhere. And travels in its own streamlined snap-on case–with retractable carrying handle. Weighs a mere 8lbs.

Five-year guarantee. The new Figurematic now carries the same generous parts warranty as do all Smith-Corona portable typewriters and adding machines.

Try it at your dealers now. Any office-equipment dealer or department store will be glad to demonstrate exactly what this low-cost, all-electric adding machine can do. Tax computation. Inventories. Purchase totals. Budgets. Statistical analysis. Even school work.

You may even forget how to add, subtract and multiply. But we figure you've got better things to do with your time anyway.

the new Smith-Corona Figurematic

The Cold War–Battlefield Vietnam

Fearful that a "domino effect" would see an uncontained spread of communism across the world, the US committed to supporting South Vietnam, financially and militarily, during its 30-year-long bloody civil war against North Vietnam (the Viet Cong). At the same time, communist China and USSR were jointly aiding the Viet Cong's invasion southward. Vietnam had become a Cold War battlefield.

America's involvement in Vietnam (known in Vietnam as the American War) drastically intensified during the mid-'60s when President Johnson sent hundreds of thousands of US combat forces into battle. By the end of 1967, 458,600 American troops were fighting alongside South Vietnamese and Allied forces.[1]

Right: 9th Marines take cover at Con Thien, 1967.
Below: USAF with AIM-7E Sparrow missiles, 1967

The US Airforce regularly attacked Viet Cong hideouts with toxic chemical weapons, attempting to clear the jungle's dense foliage. 20 million gallons of herbicides, including Agent Orange, were sprayed over Vietnam, Laos and Cambodia during the decade.[2] Cancers, birth defects and other serious health issues resulted.

As the war dragged on, US soldiers were beset with rising casualties, physical and psychological stress, and increasing distrust of their own government. Forced to fight a war they didn't believe in, morale among the draftees was low. Drug usage became rampant. It is estimated up to 50% of US soldiers experimented with marijuana, opium and heroin, cheaply available on the streets of Saigon. US military hospitals would later report drug abuse victims far outnumbered actual war casualties.

[1] americanwarlibrary.com/vietnam/vwatl.htm.   [2] history.com/topics/vietnam-war/agent-orange-1.

Anti-Vietnam Protests

By 1967, growing anti-war sentiment was spreading throughout America and major cities across the world. Media coverage exposed the brutality of the war and the true number of casualties. Boosted by those opposed to the draft, which drew unfairly from the minorities and the less wealthy, African Americans, religious leaders, veterans, soldiers and parents, joined students and intellectuals in the Peace Movement.

Protesters sit-in at the Pentagon Mall Entrance, watched by military police, 21st Oct 1967.

Right: Anti-Vietnam War Protest in Washington, DC. 21st Oct 1967.

On 21st Oct 1967, in one of the largest anti-war demonstrations to date, over 100,000 gathered at the Lincoln Memorial in Washington, DC. Roughly 50,000 marched from there to the Pentagon to continue their protest. Clashes with US Marshals and police resulted in the arrest of nearly 650 protesters.

An anti-Vietnam War demonstrator offers a flower to military police on guard at the Pentagon. 21st Oct 1967, Arlington, Virginia.

The Long, Hot Summer of Riots

The anti-war protests were just one of many social change movements to rock affluent Western nations in 1967. The women's movement, the students movement, the gay rights movement and the environmental movement escalated from previous years, changing our view of the world, and ultimately government policy.

In the USA, the Civil Rights protests were among the most visible of all the social change movements. Demonstrations by African Americans, their supporters, and other minorities, had been gaining momentum for the preceding ten years. By June 1967, protests reached a tipping point in what would become known as "the long, hot summer of riots".

Nearly 160 race riots broke out across the US during the three months of summer. More than 100 cities were affected, with casualties counting 83 dead, thousands injured, and swathes of destroyed property including the burning of entire neighborhoods.

12th July– Riots broke out in Newark, New Jersey, following the beating and arrest of a black taxi driver in broad daylight after he passed a parked police car. Angry crowds hurled bricks and Molotov cocktails at the police station, while looters attacked nearby stores. After five days of looting, arson, and rioting, the US National Guard arrived to assist the local police. More than 1,000 were arrested, with 700 injured and 26 people killed.

23rd–28th July– The Detroit Riots were by far the bloodiest riots of 1967, and the most deadly in US history since the Draft Riots of the American Civil War (1863).

Following a police raid on an unlicensed bar, with hundreds of patrons arrested, furious local residents rioted. The rampage continued for five days leaving 43 dead, hundreds injured, and thousands homeless from property damage. The police, US Army and National Guard were accused of indiscriminate shooting in their efforts to quell the riots.

The grievances of the Detroit rioters were many: African Americans were frustrated by the lack of jobs and promotion opportunities, and furious at the continued segregation of housing. The riots forced local and state governments to enact positive legislative changes, adjusting public policy on employment practices and fair housing.

23rd–30th July– The Puerto Rican Riots of New York's East Harlem district erupted after a knife-carrying Puerto Rican man was repeatedly shot and killed by a plain-clothed white policeman. Over 1,000 police gathered throughout the week to contain the Hispanic and African American rioters. Looting as far south as Fifth Avenue was reported.

Puerto Ricans demonstrate for civil rights at City Hall, New York City, 1967.

Advertisement

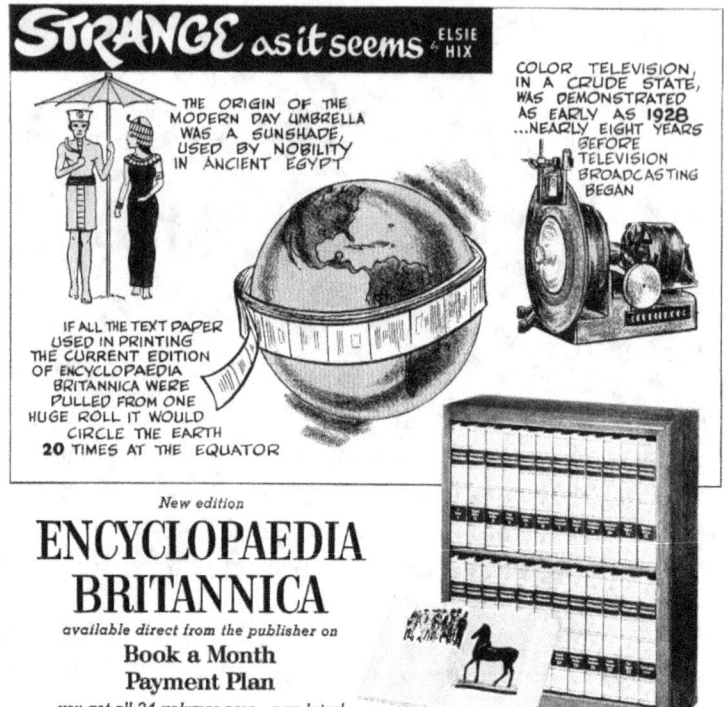

New edition
ENCYCLOPAEDIA BRITANNICA
available direct from the publisher on
Book a Month Payment Plan
you get all 24 volumes now...pay later!

The latest edition of Britannica–the greatest treasury of knowledge ever published–is the greatest in our almost 200-year publishing history. An *enormous printing* materially reduces our costs and under a remarkable direct-from-the-publisher plan, we pass these benefits on to you. All 24 handsome volumes of this world-renowned reference library will be delivered to your home NOW *direct from the publisher*. You pay later at a cost so low it is as easy as buying a book a month!

Equivalent to a library of 1,000 books. Encyclopaedia Britannica is the most valuable gift you can give yourself and your family–the priceless gift of knowledge. Information on every subject significant to mankind is contained in its new edition. It is equivalent to a library of 1,000 books, bringing you the knowledge and authority of world-recognized leaders in every field.

Just think of a subject–and you'll find it in Encyclopaedia Britannica– whether it is information on the rules of a sport, the background of a religion, how to build a brick arch in a fireplace, or the science of launching a guided missile. The new Britannica almost "televises" information to you, with over 22,000 magnificent photographs, maps and drawings. In every respect, Britannica is the largest and most complete reference set published in America, containing more than 28,000 pages and over 36,000,000 words.

Symbol of a good home. Encyclopaedia Britannica cannot help but have a lasting effect on you as well as on the growth and development of your children in school and later life. Benjamin Franklin said, "An investment in knowledge pays the best interest," and Britannica gives you the accumulated knowledge of the world in clear, easy-to-read language and superb illustrations. It is essential in every home where education is valued and respected.

Advertisement

The sophisticated camera that's "simple" minded.

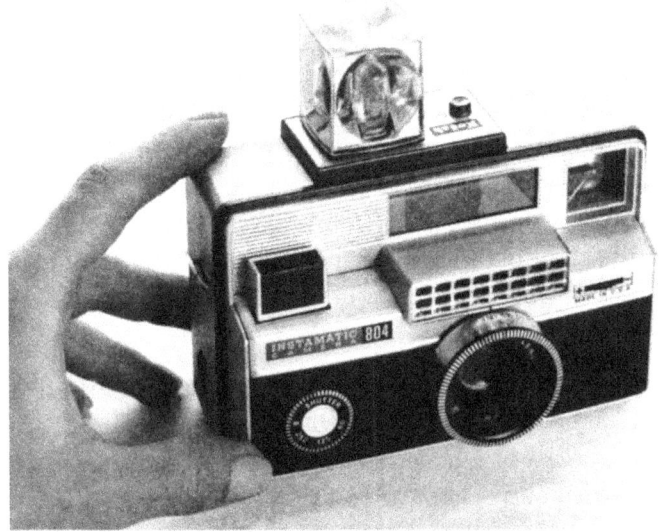

The KODAK INSTAMATIC 804 Camera knows it all—and makes it easy. You never do any figuring. A built-in computer does it for you, setting the correct exposure automatically. For daylight *and* for flash.

Practically everything else about the 804 is automatic, too. Automatically, it adjusts for the speed of the film, advances the film after each shot, tells you when to use flash, switches to flash speed when you pop on a flashcube, and turns the cube for the next shot. To load the 804, just drop in the film cartridge. To focus, use either the rangefinder or the quick "zone" settings. The lens is a sharp, fast f/2.8.

Shouldn't you be clicking with the automated precision camera that lets you concentrate on the fun side of photography? Less than $130 at your Kodak dealer's.

Price subject to change without notice.

The <u>Kodak Instamatic</u> 804 Camera

The sophisticated camera that's "simple" minded.

The Kodak Instamatic 804 Camera knows it all—and makes it easy. You never do any figuring. A built-in computer does it for you, setting the correct exposure automatically. For daylight *and* for flash.

Practically everything else about the 804 is automatic, too. Automatically, it adjusts for the speed of the film, advances the film after each shot, tells you when to use flash, switches to flash speed when you pop on a flashcube, and turns the cube for the next shot. To load the 804, just drop in the film cartridge. To focus, use either the rangefinder or the quick "zone" settings. The lens is a sharp, fast $f/2.8$.

Shouldn't you be clicking with the automated precision camera that lets you concentrate on the fun side of photography? Less than $130 at your Kodak Dealer's.

China's Cultural Revolution

The Great Proletarian Cultural Revolution is remembered as one of the bloodiest eras in China's recent history. Conceived by Chairman Mao Zedong, the revolution aimed to "rid" the country of "enemy" elements and protect Mao's reign as dictator for life.

One year earlier, in an attempt to eliminate his critics, Mao called for a mass revolution at all levels of society. Without clear direction on who the enemy was, or how to purge them, students from primary to university levels took up the challenge. Known as "Red Guards", they denounced their own teachers and school administrators as bourgeois traitors. Others followed, denouncing friends, neighbors, and even family members. Those incriminated met with public humiliation, torture and murder. The police were ordered not to intervene.

By 1967, revolutionary committees were being formed nationwide to seize power in factories, offices, and local government. Although some rallied to the call of Mao's revolution, many were looking for personal gain. Battles between rival committees broke out in virtually every city.

The chaos and violence continued without clear direction. With the revolution spiraling out of control, the army was eventually called to restore order. Although Mao officially ended the Cultural Revolution in 1969, the attacks continued until his death in 1976. The revolution resulted in the deaths of an estimated 20 million people. The ruling party ultimately declared the Cultural Revolution a "catastrophe" which had resulted in "disastrous consequences".

Above and right: Low ranking party officials being criticized by Red Guards and forced parade through the streets wearing "accusation placards". Harbin, China.

The Six-Day War in the Middle East   5th-10th June 1967

On 5th June, without warning, Israeli troops attacked the Egyptian-occupied Gaza Strip and the Sinai Peninsula. Simultaneously, Israeli air forces bombed Egypt's airfields, swiftly crippling Egypt's Air Force.

Egypt's allies, Syria and Jordan, rushed to assist their neighbor. However, with the element of surprise and superior air power, Israel quickly decimated the Arab forces. The battle would become known as the Six-Day War.

Israel conquered the Sinai Peninsula and Gaza Strip from Egypt, the Golan Heights from Syria, and the West Bank and East Jerusalem from Jordan. For the first time in nearly 2,000 years, Jerusalem's holy Jewish sites were back under Jewish control.

Defense Minister Moshe Dayan, Chief of staff Yitzhak Rabin, Gen. Rehavam Zeevi (R) And Gen. Narkis enter the old city of Jerusalem, 7th June 1967.

Casualties for the Arab nations counted more than 18,000 lives lost, against the loss of 700 Israeli lives. Hundreds of thousands of displaced Palestinians fled the conquered lands.

The Jewish state was finally in control of lands it claimed a historical rightful ownership of– lands the Arab nations also maintained belonged to them.

Israeli troops advance, Golan Heights, 10th June 1967.

Since the creation of the Israel in 1948, the fledgling state has battled numerous military and political conflicts with its Arab neighbors. The legacy of the Six-Day War continues to be felt today, as the threat of a larger and deadlier war endures.

Advertisement

It's a tape recorder. It uses a quick-loading cartridge that plays for 1 hr. It's battery-operated, it's compact, it's solid-state. It's the Wollensak 4100.

Always on the job—the only recorder that has everything! Comes complete: dynamic microphone, 3 "Scotch" Brand Tape cartridges, batteries, carrying case, shoulder strap, accessory cord—no extras to buy. Goes everywhere, records and plays on its own batteries. On the job, at school, in study or lecture hall... taking notes, recording lectures or interviews. And wherever the fun is—at home, at the beach, parties—it's your private ear, ready to listen and play back at your command. Compact—weighs 3lbs. Cartridges snap in—no threading. One-function control. Remote control mike switch. VU meter monitors recording level and battery life. Constant capstan-drive $1^7/_8$ IPS tape speed. Get the recorder that's complete for work or fun: the new Wollensak 4100... at your Wollensak dealer.

Advertisement

86 glittering spots like these show you what makes London the springboard for Europe.

Via BEA.
Europe's biggest airline.

Clever way to lengthen your European vacation: shorten your travel time. By flying British European Airways all over Europe, the Mediterranean, the Middle East.

When your transatlantic flight lands you in London, BEA will be ready to fly you to any one of 86 exciting cities.

It's coverage like this that makes BEA Europe's biggest airline.

BEA flew 7,000,000 passengers last year. And over 400,000 of these were Americans.

Americans feel at home on BEA, and at 610 mph, "feeling at home" is the kind of calm, comforting feeling you like to have.

The equipment, the decor, the personnel have a "British cousin" look about them that put you at your ease.

The stewardesses are friendly, pretty, couldn't do enough for you.

The airplanes? Smart. Comfortable. Relaxing. (Newest among them are the triple-jet Tridents. Mighty Rolls-Royce engines at the rear to leave noise behind.)

We couldn't begin to tell you about all of BEA's cities.

But your travel agent can. See him. Or visit any airline office.

And ask to be booked on BEA.

General Sales Agents in U.S.A. and Canada: BOAC

BRITISH EUROPEAN AIRWAYS

1967 in Cinema and Film

1967 is widely recognized as a groundbreaking year for cinema, with several landmark films shattering the taboos of the time. While experimental cinematography ushered in a new era of Hollywood artistic freedoms, younger audiences clamored for radical themes previously shunned by the movie houses.

Movies became more defiant, cynical, anti-establishment, violent, and sexually explicit. Anti-hero misfits were celebrated (*Bonnie and Clyde, The Dirty Dozen, Cool Hand Luke*). Drug usage and its psychedelic effects were flaunted (*The Trip, Valley of the Dolls*). Cursing became acceptable (*In Cold Blood, I'll Never Forget What's 'is Name, Ulysses*).

Faye Dunaway in *Bonnie and Clyde* (Warner Bros. 1967).

Katharine Houghton and Sidney Poitier in *Guess Who's Coming to Dinner* (Columbia Pictures, 1967).

Confronting social norms, *In the Heat of the Night* and *Guess Who's Coming to Dinner* tackled racial prejudice, while *The Graduate* examined middle-class social and sexual values.

Dustin Hoffman in 1968.

1967 film debuts

Faye Dunaway	Hurry Sundown
Dustin Hoffman	The Tiger Makes Out
Anthony Hopkins	The White Bus
Richard Pryor	The Busy Body
Gene Wilder	Bonnie and Clyde
Michael York	The Taming of the Shrew
Harvey Keitel	Who's That Knocking at My Door

* From en.wikipedia.org/wiki/1967_in_film.

Top Grossing Films of the Year

1	The Graduate	United Artists/Embassy	$43,100,000
2	Guess Who's Coming to Dinner	Columbia Pictures	$25,500,000
3	Bonnie and Clyde	Warner Bros.	$22,000,000
4	The Dirty Dozen	Metro-Goldwyn-Mayer	$20,100,000
5	Valley of the Dolls	20th Century Fox	$20,000,000
6	To Sir, with Love	Columbia Pictures	$19,100,000
7	You Only Live Twice	Artists/Eon Production	$18,000,000
8	Thoroughly Modern Millie	Universal Pictures	$14,700,000
9	The Jungle Book	Walt Disney/Buena Vista	$13,000,000
10	Camelot	Warner Bros.	$12,300,000

* From en.wikipedia.org/wiki/1967_in_film by box office gross in the USA.

The critically acclaimed film *The Graduate* achieved 7 Academy Award nominations, launching the career of the young and unknown Dustin Hoffman. Several A-list actors were turned down for the role, lacking the vulnerability that Hoffman possessed. Hoffman was paid just $20,000. After tax and some months of expenses, he filed for unemployment benefits.

Clint Eastwood as "Blondie" in *The Good, The Bad and The Ugly* (United Artists, 1966).

During the '60s, the genre of "Spaghetti Westerns" continued to rise. These Italian productions, filmed in various European locations, stared a host of European actors with fading, or up-and-coming Hollywood stars. Although largely low budget and low profit, Sergio Leone's hugely successful *Dollar* series, starring Clint Eastwood, (*A Fistful of Dollars, For a Few Dollars More,* and *The Good, The Bad and The Ugly),* were all released in the USA during 1967.

Hollywood also had to compete with rising talent from foreign film directors and foreign stars, such as Brigitte Bardot (France), Sophia Loren (Italy), Sean Connery and Richard Burton (England).

Brigitte Bardot.

Sophia Loren.

Espionage Films of 1967

You Only Live Twice (United Artists, 1967).   The Karate Killers (MGM. 1967).

Combining thrilling action with exotic locations, a dose of escapism and political intrigue or science fiction, the Spy Genre or Espionage films grew in popularity during the mid-'60s.

The Double Man (Warner Bros. 1967).   The Deadly Affair (Columbia, 1967).

Advertisement

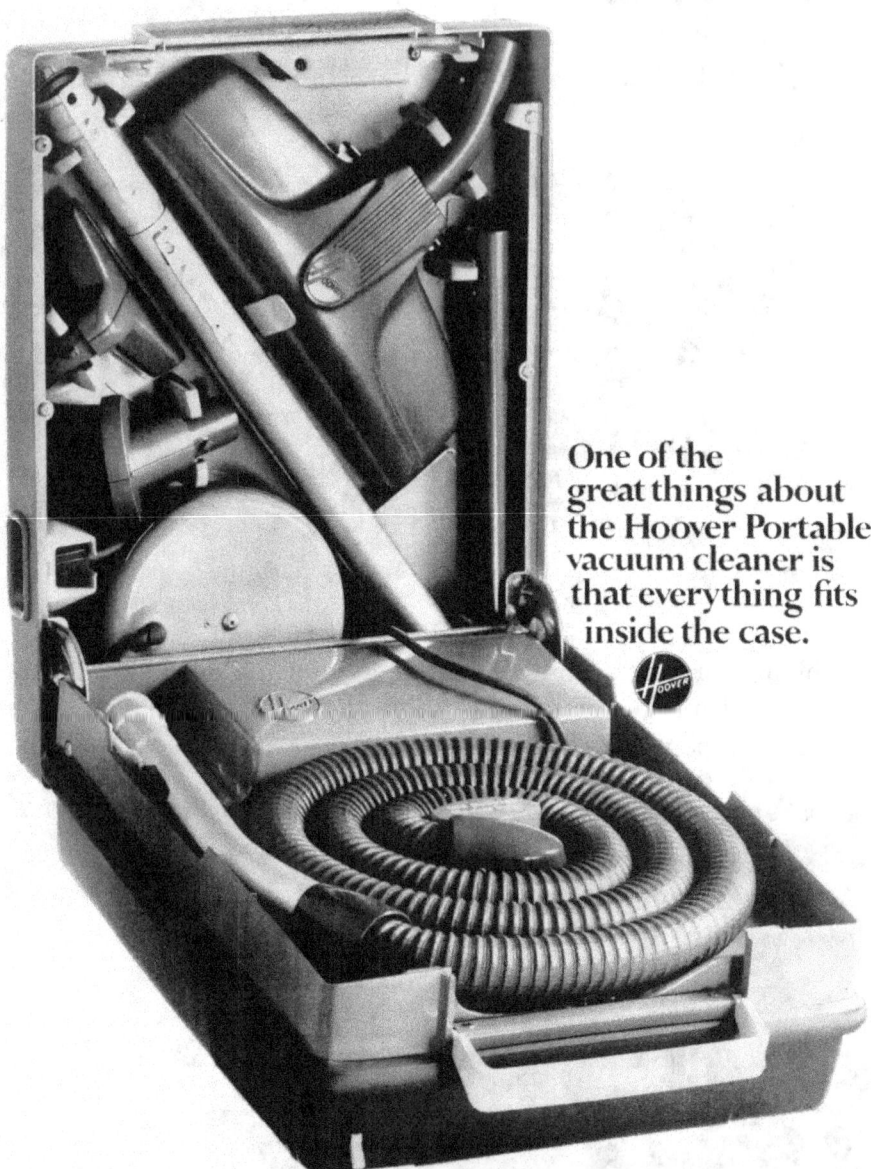

One of the great things about the Hoover Portable vacuum cleaner is that everything fits inside the case.

Some of the other great things: all the attachments you need, a telescoping wand, an attached Tufflex hose, full Hoover cleaning power. See the Hoover Portable at your Hoover dealer. It's really great.

One of the great things about the Hoover Portable vacuum cleaner is that everything fits inside the case.

Some of the other great things: all the attachments you need, a telescoping wand, an attached Tufflex hose, full Hoover cleaning power.
See the Hoover Portable at your Hoover dealer. It's really great.

Musical Memories

The "British Invasion" of the mid-'60s delivered a flood of British talent to prominence around the world, pushing them to the top of the music charts. UK artists like The Yardbirds, The Who, The Kinks, The Rolling Stones, and mega-band The Beatles, wrote their own songs and played their own music. They experimented with exotic instruments and sounds, feedback and distortion, spiced with a good dose of marijuana and LSD, paving the way for the next wave of psychedelic pop artists.

By 1967, American bands were coming into their own. Inspired by the music of the Brits, mixed with new psychedelic sounds and feel-good rhythms, The Beach Boys, The Monkeys, The Mamas & The Papas, and others began to climb the charts.

The Beach Boys, 1967.

The Temptations, 1968.

Unaffected by the British influence, Motown continued to pump out the hits. This Detroit independent record label represented top selling soul artists including The Supremes, Marvin Gaye, Stevie Wonder, Jackson 5, The Temptations, and Four Tops.

12th Feb–Mick Jagger, Keith Richards and Marianne Faithful arrested for possession of drugs.

31st Jul–Keith Richards and Mick Jagger ended a one month jail sentence.

9th Nov– First issue of *Rolling Stone* magazine was issued.

9th Dec–Jim Morrison was arrested for disturbing the peace while preforming on stage in Connecticut.

9th Dec– Otis Redding was killed in a plane crash, three days after recording *Sittin' on the Dock of the Bay,* aged 26.

1st May– Elvis Presley and Priscilla Beaulieu married in Las Vegas.

San Francisco's Summer of Love

"If you're going to San Francisco, be sure to wear flowers in your hair"[1]

In the summer of '67, around 100,000 mostly young adults descended on the Haight Ashbury district of San Francisco in search of utopia—where peace and love could save the world. For some it would be a profound experience which would change the course of their lives. For others it would be a few weeks or months of debauchery and chaos. Sex and drugs flowed freely, and of course there was music.

Monterey International Pop Festival poster by Tom Wilkes, May 1967.

[1] *San Francisco,* written by John Phillips to promote the Monterey International Pop Festival. Sung by Scott McKenzie, May 1967.

16th-18th June– *Monterey Pop* is considered America's first major rock festival, and the public coming-out for the flower-power and flower-children hippie movements. An estimated 200,000 came to watch Jimi Hendrix, The Who, Grateful Dead, The Animals, Jefferson Airplane, The Byrds, Otis Redding, The Mamas & the Papas, little-known Janis Joplin, and more. The eclectic line up also included Ravi Shankar (India) and Hugh Masekala (South Africa). The event's organization, covering medical care, food, security, and volunteers, set the standard for future music festivals.

Left: Janis Joplin, 1969. Below: Jimi Hendrix, 1967.

Jefferson Airplane at *Fantasy Fair*, 1967.

The Doors.

10th-11th June– The *Fantasy Fair and Magic Mountain Music Festival* was attended by a crowd of 40,000. On a mountainside in Marin County, CA., The Doors played to their first large audience. Headline acts included Canned Heat, Dionne Warwick, The Byrds, The Grass Roots, and Jefferson Airplane. Hells Angels Motorcycle Club members acted as security guards, in what was a well managed and peaceful event. The considerate crowd cleaned up all litter before leaving.

During the three months of summer, numerous Be-Ins and music festivals popped up across America, from Denver to Portland, and in Central Park, NY. The hippy mantra spread far and wide–from the UK's *International Love-In Festival* (London), the *Festival of the Flower Children* (Woburn) and the *Festival of Music* (Hastings), to festivals in Canada, Italy, Netherlands, Prague, Belgium and Brazil.

Hair, the musical, debuted off-Broadway on 17th Oct 1967, moving to Broadway's Biltmore Theatre six months later. Exploring themes from hippie culture, the show promoted sexual and spiritual freedoms, drug use, and rejection of materialism and conservatism. Several of the musical's songs have become hippie anthems.

Promoting the musical *Hair* in Finland by the cast of Popteatteri, Helsinki.

Advertisement

It combines an Ampex Stereo tape recorder/player and AM/FM stereo receiver.

Its simplicity enables you to tape a musical library right off the air—with incredible ease.

It has such innovations as automatic reverse for uninterrupted listening.

It gives you professional quality sound with a choice of Ampex Speakers.

Its walnut finish and sliding doors say quality in any decor.

It's called the Ampex 985 Music Center.

It combines an Ampex Stereo tape recorder/player and AM/FM stereo receiver.
Its simplicity enables you to tape a musical library right off the air—with incredible ease.
It has such innovations as automatic reverse for uninterrupted listening.
It gives you professional quality sound with a choice of Ampex Speakers.
Its walnut finish and sliding doors say quality in any decor.
It's called the Ampex 985 Music Center.

It's the end.

Wes Wilson's Psychedelic Concert Posters

The psychedelic posters created by San Francisco artist Wes Wilson spearheaded the hippy aesthetic of flowing lava lamp designs with bubbly lettering in kaleidoscopic colors. Inspired by the freedom of the Art Nouveau, Wilson's ideas for turning posters into expressive artforms were a radical departure from the usual plain and legible poster typography.

During 1966-'67, Wilson created 40 posters for the Fillmore Auditorium in San Francisco, making the venue a focal point for American psychedelic music and countercultures.

Life magazine showcased a montage of Wilson's posters on the 1st Sep 1967 cover.

Bill Graham presents in San Francisco. Jefferson Airplane, Grateful Dead. Fri. 12 Aug. Sat. 13 Aug. Fillmore Auditorium.

Bill Graham presents in San Francisco. Otis Rush, Grateful Dead, The Canned Heat Blues Band. Fri. Sat. 9pm $3.00. Sun. 2-7pm $2.00. At the Fillmore.

Bill Graham presents in San Francisco. Buffalo Springfield, Steve Miller Blues Band. All Alive at the Fillmore. And Freedom Highway. April 28,29,30.

1967 Billboard Top 30 Songs

	Artist	Song Title
1	Lulu	To Sir With Love
2	The Box Tops	The Letter
3	Bobbie Gentry	Ode to Billie Joe
4	The Association	Windy
5	The Monkees	I'm a Believer
6	The Doors	Light My Fire
7	Frank & Nancy Sinatra	Somethin' Stupid
8	The Turtles	Happy Together
9	The Young Rascals	Groovin'
10	Frankie Valli	Can't Take My Eyes off You

The Supremes, 1967.

Frank & Nancy Sinatra, 1966.

Lulu, 1965.

The Monkees, 1966.

	Artist	Song Title
11	The Music Explosion	Little Bit O' Soul
12	Tommy James and the Shondells	I Think We're Alone Now
13	Aretha Franklin	Respect
14	Stevie Wonder	I Was Made to Love Her
15	Bobby Vee	Come Back When You Grow Up
16	The Buckinghams	Kind of a Drag
17	Arthur Conley	Sweet Soul Music
18	The Soul Survivors	Expressway to Your Heart
19	Sam & Dave	Soul Man
20	The Association	Never My Love

Aretha Franklin, 1968.   Stevie Wonder, 1967.

	Artist	Song Title
21	Jay & the Techniques	Apples, Peaches, Pumpkin Pie
22	Every Mother's Son	Come on Down to My Boat
23	Strawberry Alarm Clock	Incense and Peppermints
24	The Rolling Stones	Ruby Tuesday
25	Vikki Carr	It Must Be Him
26	The Supremes	Love Is Here and Now You're Gone
27	Buffalo Springfield	For What It's Worth
28	Brenton Wood	Gimme Little Sign
29	The Supremes	The Happening
30	The Beatles	All You Need Is Love

* From the *Billboard* top 30 singles of 1967.

Advertisement

Fashion choices from the Montgomery Ward catalog, Summer 1967.

Fashion Trends of the 1960s

The 1960s was an exciting decade for fashion, with new trends that caught on and transformed quickly. It was a decade of fashion extremes driven by shifting social movements, radical youth, rebelliousness and rejection of traditions.

In the early '60s, fashion was content to continue the conservative classic style of the previous decade. The elegant sheath dress and tailored skirt-suits were favored for day wear.

And for dinners and cocktails, '50s style hourglass dresses were still common. Skirts stayed long, full and very lady-like. Matching accessories such as gloves, hat, scarves, jewelry and stiletto or kitten-heel shoes were mandatory.

Jacqueline Kennedy may have been the US first lady for only three years, but as first lady of fashion, her iconic status has endured till this day. Always impeccably groomed, her every move was analyzed and cataloged by newspaper and style magazines for every lady to follow.

Here are some of her classic iconic looks:
- Tailored skirt-suit with three-quarter sleeve length box jacket and matching pill box hat.
- Sheath dress with white gloves and low-heel pump shoes.
- A-line dress, long or short, with three-quarter length gloves for evening.

However, the conservative elegance of the early '60s would soon be energetically and wholeheartedly rejected. The decade of the 1960s belonged to the British youth centered around London, who would capture the world's attention with their free spirits, energy, music, and style. By 1967, the "British Invasion" had exploded on the world, introducing us to the "Mods" and the "Swinging Sixties". These movements defined the era and changed the world of fashion forever.

The Mods were clean-cut college boys who favored slim-fitting suits or short jackets over turtle-neck or buttoned up polo shirts. Pants were pipe-legged with no cuffs, worn over pointed polished shoes or ankle boots.

The Mods were obsessed with Italian fashion, French haircuts, alternative music and Vespa scooters.

Mod fashion was adopted by the many British Invasion bands of the mid-'60s: The Kinks, The Who, The Yardbirds, The Rolling Stones and The Beatles all adopted the Mod look in the early part of their careers.

For the girls, London designer Mary Quant created fashion for the young and free-spirited woman. Credited for inventing the mini-skirt, Quant considered her youthful designs liberating, allowing women to run and move freely. Her clients were hedonistic, creative, wealthy, and sexually liberated. They helped shape the Swinging Sixties cultural revolution.

Quant's Kings Road boutique featured her trademark simple short sheath dresses in bold or floral patterns, worn with solid colored or patterned tights.

She also championed trousers for women— with choices ranging from long flared, harem, or ankle length Capris, to mid-length Bermudas and skimpy hotpants.

Below Left: Mary Quant.
Below Right: Models in Quant plastic coats and boots.

Top: Models wear Mary Quant dresses.
Above: Quant inspired street dresses.

Quant's experimental use of new materials was revolutionary. Shiny PVC raincoats came in an array of solid statement colors, matched with patent vinyl boots. Synthetic dresses paired with a range of bold, colorful plastic jewellery, handbags and accessories.

The Swinging Sixties was also the era of the first wave of British supermodels–tall, skinny, leggy young ladies who broke with the aristocratic look of earlier-generation models. With enormous eyes and quirky descriptive names, Jean Shrimpton, Twiggy and Penelope Tree were in-demand icons world-wide.

Penelope Tree for *Vogue,* October 1967.

Twiggy for *Italian Vogue,* July 1967.

Twiggy various photo shoots.

Jean Shrimpton for *Vogue*, Sept 1967.

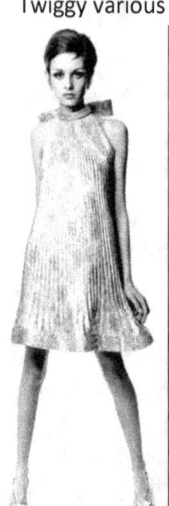   

Advertisement

Cut up, cut out, cut loose with Max Factor's California Pink-A-Pades

Two pink escapades for lips and fingertips.
Two sheer... two shimmering... too tempting!
It's the great new color adventure for summer.
Say it Pink-A-Pale (soft, feminine, fragile)
Or Pink-A-Fling (lively, zingy, daring).
Wear it either super-sheer or super-frosted.
Any way you play it, have a wild pink Pink-A-Pade!

California Pink-A-Pades by Max Faxtor

Known as the Space Age designer, French couturier André Courrèges employed geometric shapes in metallic silvers and stark whites to give his dresses futuristic forms. His revolutionary designs from the mid-'60s mixed plastics and fur with leathers and wool, accessorising with astronaut inspired helmets, goggles and flat white go-go boots.

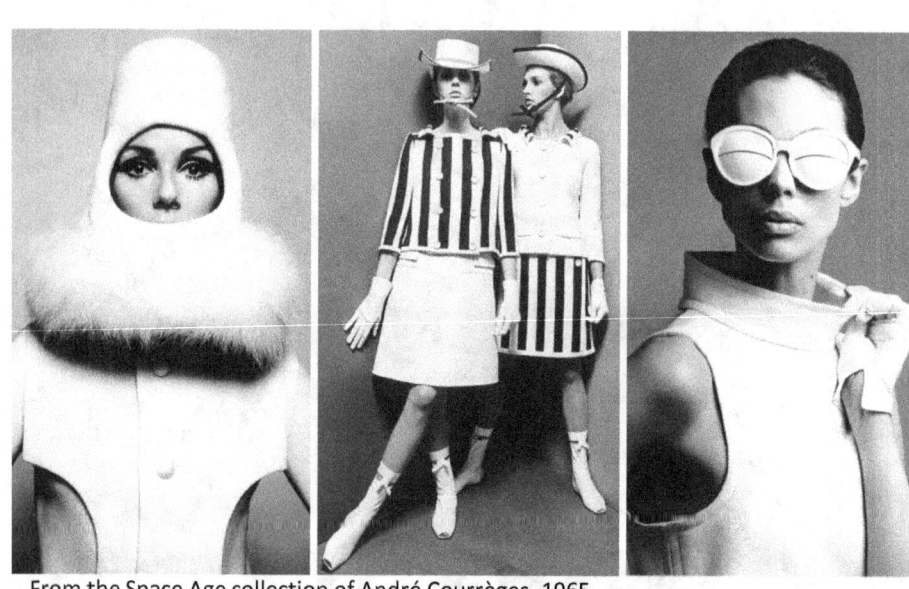

From the Space Age collection of André Courrèges, 1965.

André Courrèges' cut out dress.

Inspired by Courrèges, Space Bride by Jezebel, 1966 New York.

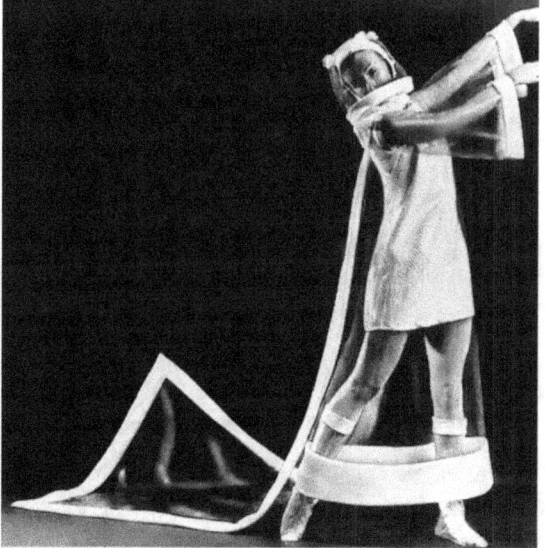

As the fashion and attitudes of swinging London spread to America and other parts of the world, the subculture became commercialized on a mass scale and began to loose its vitality. The fun loving movement morphed into the psychedelic rock and early hippie movements.

Led by musicians such as The Beatles, The Beach Boys, Pink Floyd and The Who, and fuelled by widespread use of marijuana and LSD, psychedelic fashion became an expression of the hallucinogenic experience. Bright colors, swirling patterns and kaleidoscopic floral designs adorned full flowing forms in soft fabrics.

Photo from The Beatles *Magical Mystery Tour,* 1967.

The psychedelic rock movement petered out by the end of the 1960s, but the hippie generation was only just beginning. Hippies would drive fashion forward, well into the next decade.

Advertisement

Only on TWA to California.
Your choice of 5 entrees, cooked to order.

Taste what's happened to TWA Royal Ambassador First Class at lunch or dinner time: Broiled Filet Mignon, Veal Parmigiana, Chicken Cacciatore, Double-Cut Lamb Chops, Maine Lobster Thermidor. We'll cook your choice to your order, serve it graciously and surround it with cocktails, wines, fruit, inspired desserts. It's a taste of the good life only an international airline could offer.

Enjoy it soon. It's on most TWA non-stops from Chicago to the Coast: 7 every day to Los Angeles (hi-fi and stereo included), 6 every day to San Francisco. Call Mr. Information (your travel agent) or call TWA.

Something special on TWA to New York, too. 14 non-stops a day from Chicago.

Welcome to the world of Trans World Airlines

Science and Technology

12th Jan– Dr. James H. Bedford became the first person to be cryogenically preserved. His body remains were preserved after his death, however, it is unlikely his organs have survived the test of time.

9th Apr– The first Boeing 737 took its maiden test flight, and in Dec '67, Lufthansa became the first airline company to receive a 737. The plane later became the most purchased commercial aircraft in the world.

27th Apr-29th Oct– Expo 67 was held in Montreal, Canada. The successful expo set new records for attendance, with 62 nations participating.

30th Jun– Robert Henry Lawrence, Jr. became the first African American Astronaut, when he was selected the join the crew for a series of low earth orbit mini-space station missions. He would die later the same year in a plane crash.

28th Nov– University of Cambridge astrophysics postgraduate student Jocelyn Bell discovered the first pulsars (pulsating radio source) emanating from a distant neutron star. This discovery led to a Nobel Prize (1974) being awarded to her thesis supervisor. Bell was denied the award because she was a woman and a student.

27th Jun– The world's first ATM (Automatic Teller Machine) began dispensing cash at Barclays Bank in Enfield, North London, UK.

3rd Dec– South African surgeon Dr. Christiaan Barnard performed the world's first human to human heart transplant. The transplant was successful, although the patient died 18 days later due to pneumonia.

Advertisement

Maybe this is where we should sell our new motor oil.

We have a new Detergent Oil that cleans your car's engine, a lot like a good laundry detergent cleans your clothes.

It circulates around inside your engine, and keeps dirt moving.

It doesn't let deposits settle down. (Where they can gum up the works. And cost you big repair bills.)

And because dirt is kept moving, it all goes down the drain when you change your oil.

And that isn't everything our new Detergent Oil does.

It also prevents harmful engine "varnish." (Which can form inside your engine, and clog up valves and other moving parts.)

It keeps oil screens clean longer, so your oil pump can pump oil better.

It doesn't thin out as fast from stop-and-go driving.

In fact, our new Detergent Oil is so good, it exceeds the warranty requirements of every U.S. car maker.

Our new oil's full name is Mobiloil Super 10W-40.

The '10W' means you get the easy starts and fast warm-ups of a thin number 10 winter oil.

The '40' means you get the engine protection and lower consumption of a heavy number 40 summer oil.

All of which means you get all the advantages of both, all year around, with just one oil.

Think about it.

Maybe it's time to change your oil.

Mobil
The Detergent Oil

We have a new Detergent Oil that cleans your car's engine, a lot like a good laundry detergent cleans your clothes. It circulates around inside your engine, and keeps dirt moving. It doesn't let deposits settle down. (Where they can gum up the works. And cost you big repair bills.) And because dirt is kept moving, it all goes down the drain when you change your oil.

And that isn't everything our new Detergent Oil does.

It also prevents harmful engine "varnish." (Which can form inside your engine, and clog up valves and other moving parts.) It keeps oil screens clean longer, so your oil pump can pump oil better. It doesn't thin out as fast from stop-and-go driving. In fact, our new Detergent Oil is so good, it *exceeds* the warranty requirements of every U.S. car maker.

Our new oil's *full* name is Mobiloil Super 10W-40. The '10W' means you get the easy starts and fast warm-ups of a thin number 10 winter oil. The '40' means you get the engine protection and lower consumption of a heavy number 40 summer oil.

All of which means you get all the advantages of both, all year around, with just one oil. Think about it. Maybe it's time to change your oil.

Also in Sports

26th Feb– Mario Andretti won the NASCAR Grand National at Daytona, the first time a driver born outside the US had ever won the Race.

19th Apr– Kathrine Switzer ran the Boston Marathon. Although welcomed by the other runners, the media and race organizers realized mid-race that a woman had infiltrated the prestigious men-only race. They set upon her, attempting to drag her out of the race. Protected by her team mates, Switzer finished the race, proving that women were capable of participating in sports at all levels.

28th Apr– Muhammad Ali refused induction into the US Army. He was stripped of his heavyweight boxing title and his anti-war stance resulted in a Draft Evasion conviction, a $10,000 fine, a three-year boxing ban, and five years in prison. His prison sentence was delayed during appeals, and in 1971 his conviction was overturned. Ali returned to the boxing ring in 1970.

3rd Jun– Australian Roy Emerson beat his countryman Tony Roche in the French Championships Tennis, taking his 12th and final Grand Slam title. 7th Jul– Australian John Newcombe beat German Wilhelm Bungert at Wimbledon winning his 1st of 3 Wimbledon singles titles. Newcombe would win the US National Championship singles titles later in the year. 8th Jul– USA's Billie Jean King beat UK's Anne Jones, her 2nd of 3 straight Wimbledon singles titles. King would win the US National Championship singles titles later in the year.

29th Aug– The NY Yanks won against the Boston Red Sox in 20, 4-3. At 8 hours 19 minutes, it was one of the longest games in baseball history.

Other News from 1967

2nd Jan— Actor turned politician Ronald Reagan was sworn in as Governor of California.

3rd Jan— Edward W. Brooke took his seat as the first elected African American to the US Senate (Sen-R-Mass).

26th Jan— A Chicago Blizzard dumped 23 inches of snowfall. 800 buses and 50,000 automobiles were abandoned as roads became impassable.

1st Feb— 110 separate bushfires ravaged southern Tasmania, Australia, killing 62 and leaving 7,000 people homeless.

12th Mar— General Suharto was appointed acting President of Indonesia, placing outgoing President Sukarno under house arrest. Suharto would go on to rule as President for 31 years, imprisoning or silencing his critics and opponents in order to maintain his ruthless dictatorial grip on power.

1st Apr— The National Transportation Safety Board (NTSB) was created under the Department of Transportation to tackle the problem of safety on the roads. Within a few years, shatter-resistant windshields, safety belts, head rests, and other safety requirements would become standard.

21st Apr— Svetlana Allilueva, the daughter of Joseph Stalin, arrived in New York City after defecting to the USA.

21st Apr— The Greek civilian government was ousted in a coup d'etat that placed the country under seven years of a far-right military dictatorship.

30th May– Argentinian author Gabriel García Márquez's "One Hundred Years of Solitude" was published in Buenos Aires. The novel brought Márquez many awards, including the 1982 Nobel Prize for Literature.

3rd Sep– Sweden switched to driving on the right-hand side of road after decades of driving on the left.

8th Aug– The Association of Southeast Asian Nations (ASEAN) was formed when leaders from Indonesia, Malaysia, Philippines, Singapore & Thailand signed the ASEAN Declaration. Now with ten member states, the association promotes peace and economic growth in the region.

2nd Oct– Thurgood Marshall was sworn in as America's first African American Justice of the Supreme Court.

9th Oct– Guerrilla leader Che Guevara was killed by CIA agents following his capture in Bolivia.

17th Dec– Australia's Prime Minister, Harold Holt, vanished while swimming near Melbourne. His body was never found.

Advertisement

Join the cola dropouts.
You get a whole new feeling with Wink.

Cola was never like this. You don't just drink Wink. You feel it.
A million liquid diamonds turn on all at once. A tintinnabulating tingle wipes out your thirst. And your taste will tell your mind... Wink is where it's at.

Canada Dry makes it.
Now in diet too.

Advertisement

Jet to her side via Delta... It's your stateside duty!

Jet to her side via Delta... It's your stateside duty!

Making plans for heading home? Then, get set to join the jet set stateside! Step up to Delta now, and take advantage of those extra special 50% Jet Military Standby Fares!

Buy your Delta ticket overseas or within 6 hours after U.S. arrival and save the domestic tax. See your Base Transportation Office, nearest Travel Agent or Delta office.

Under 22? Get a guaranteed reservation on the flight you want at 1/3 off with Delta's Youth Fare Plan. Good noon Monday to noon Friday, and noon Saturday to noon Sunday. Your military I.D. card accepted as proof of age.

Examples of Delta's low Standby Fares:
San Francisco–Delta...$45.24, San Francisco–Atlanta ...$64.25, Los Angeles–Dallas...$36.25, Los Angeles–New Orleans...$50.80, New York–New Orleans...$36.20, New York–Houston...$44.60, New York–Atlanta...$24.85, Philadelphia–New Orleans...$34.00, Philadelphia–Houston...$42.30, Philadelphia–Atlanta...$22.45

DELTA   the air line with the BIG JETS

Famous People Born in 1967

10th Feb– Laura Dern, American actress.

20th Feb– Kurt Cobain, American rock singer-songwriter (Nirvana) (d.1994).

23rd Feb– Tamsin Greig, English actress.

27th Feb– Willem-Alexander, King of the Netherlands (2013-present).

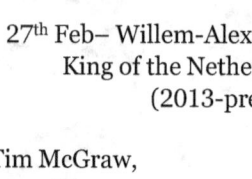

1st May– Tim McGraw, American country musician & actor.

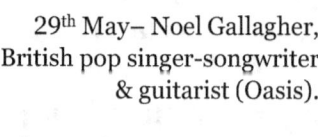

29th May– Noel Gallagher, British pop singer-songwriter & guitarist (Oasis).

3rd Jun– Anderson Cooper, American reporter & TV presenter (CNN).

12th Jun– Frances O'Connor, English-Australian actress.

20th Jun– Nicole Kidman, Australian-American actress.

1st Jul– Pamela Anderson, Canadian-American actress & Playboy playmate.

16th Jul– Will Ferrell, American comedian.

23rd Jul– Philip Seymour Hoffman, American actor (d.2014).

25th Jul– Matt LeBlanc, American actor.

6th Sep– Macy Gray [Natalie McIntyre], American singer-songwriter.

7th Sep– Leslie Jones, American comedian & actress.

8th Sep– James Packer, Australian businessman.

18th Jul– Vin Diesel [Mark Sinclair], American actor.

11th Sep– Harry Connick Jr, American singer & actor.

21st Sep– Faith Hill [Audrey Faith Perry], American singer.

28th Sep– Mira Sorvino, American actress.

5th Oct– Guy Pearce, Anglo-Australian actor.

7th Oct– Toni Braxton, American R&B singer-songwriter.

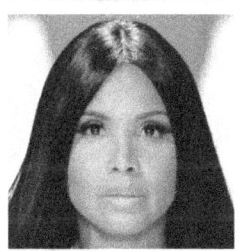

26th Oct– Keith Urban, New Zealand-Australian singer.

28th Oct– Julia Roberts, American actress.

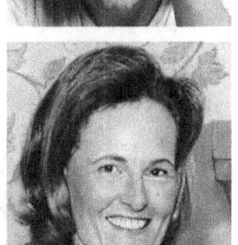

28th Oct– Sophie, Hereditary Princess of Liechtenstein.

31st Oct– Vanilla Ice [Robert Van Winkle], American rapper (Ice Ice Baby) & actor.

1st Nov– Tina Arena, Australian pop singer & songwriter.

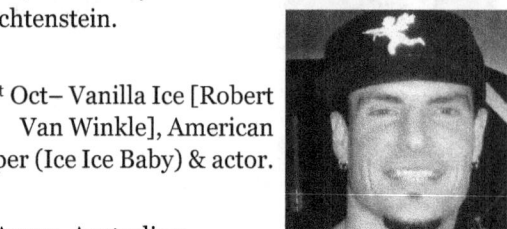

7th Nov– David Guetta, French songwriter, DJ & record producer.

13th Nov– Jimmy Kimmel, American TV host & producer.

22nd Nov– Boris Becker, German tennis player.

22nd Nov– Mark Ruffalo, American actor.

13th Dec– Jamie Foxx, American actor, comedian & musician.

23rd Dec– Carla Bruni, Italian-French model & singer-songwriter.

Advertisement

Step into the wonderful new world of frozen foods

It's a world of tasty casseroles, soufflés that can't fail, luxurious seafoods, an unmatched variety of vegetable dishes. All instantly available from your refrigerator or freezer.

It's a world that gives you time to live more fully, do more, and at the same time serve your family and friends dishes that, far from being bland, or tinny, or dull, are truly excellent.

Stouffer's, the leading quality line of frozen prepared foods, gives you welcome variety and flexibility in your meal planning, even on crowded, busy days. And most days are. You now spend a daily average of just 90 minutes in the kitchen, as against the four or five hours your mother needed. Frozen prepared foods now appear on the table several times a week in the average home. Even the best cooks serve them.

When you have quality brands like Stouffer's you can serve them regularly—with confidence.

So step into the wonderful new world of frozen foods. See how easy it becomes to plan appetizing meals for almost any situation and any occasion. Stouffer's offers 27 superb dishes. Vegetables, casseroles, special entrees for special occasions. Each is a favorite from the recipe collection of Stouffer's famous restaurants. They're in your grocer's freezer now. Enjoy them soon.

Stouffer's Frozen Foods

1967 in Numbers

Census Statistics [1]

- Population of the world   3.48 billion
- Population in the United States   203.9 million
- Population in the United Kingdom   54.87 million
- Population in Canada   20.32 million
- Population in Australia   11.90 million
- Average age for marriage of women   20.6 years old
- Average age for marriage of men   23.1 years old
- Average family income USA $7,200 per year
- Unemployment rate USA   3.8 %

Costs of Goods [2]

- Average home — $20,994
- Average new car — $2,750
- Daily paper — $0.10
- A gallon of gasoline — $0.32
- Butter — $0.75 per pound
- A gallon of milk — $1.03
- Apples, Delicious — $0.39 per 3 pounds
- Beef, London broil — $0.89 per pound
- Sliced ham — $0.69 per pound
- Lettuce, iceberg — $0.19 each
- Fresh eggs — $0.55 per dozen
- Potatoes — $0.10 per pound
- Soup, Campbells can — $0.15
- Movie ticket — $1.25

1 Figures taken from worldometers.info/world-population, US National Center for Health Statistics, Divorce and Divorce Rates US (cdc.gov/nchs/data/series/sr_21/sr21_029.pdf) and United States Census Bureau, Historical Marital Status Tables (census.gov/data/tables/time-series/demo/families/marital.html).
2 Figures from thepeoplehistory.com, mclib.info/reference/local-history & dqydj.com/historical-home-prices/.

Advertisement

BOOTS New Wide Tread tires from Goodyear

You *could* buy Goodyear's new Wide Boots because their tread is almost one-third wider than the tread on ordinary tires. Or because they start faster. Stop quicker. Handle surer. Corner safer.

You *could* buy Goodyear's new Wide Boots because they're made much like a racing tire. Squat. Broad shouldered. With a strong cord set at a low angle for less heat buildup and longer wear. With a tread of Tufsyn rubber—the toughest rubber Goodyear ever built into a tire.

Or you could buy Goodyear's new Wide Boots just because they look great.

Advertisement

Honda shapes the world of wheels

You've got to hand it to Honda. New designs. New colors. Altogether 20 models to put a glint in your eye. That famous four-stroke engine takes everything in stride. Won five out of five '66 Grand Prix Championships, 50cc to 500cc. A world's record. With Honda, performance counts as well as style. And that tells it like it is. Any questions? See your local Honda dealer for a safety demonstration ride.

Honda

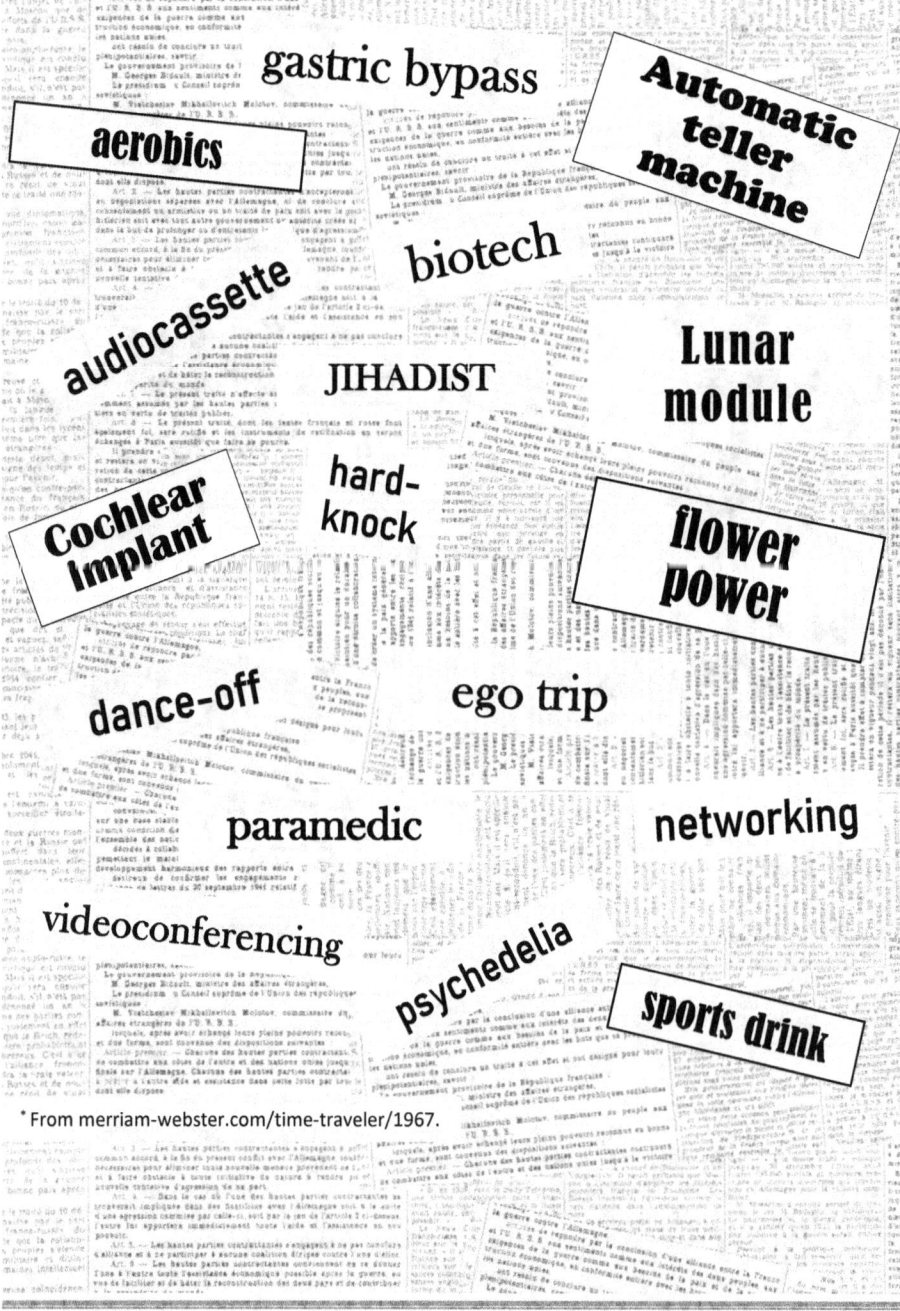

A heartfelt plea from the author:

I sincerely hope you enjoyed reading this book and that it brought back many fond memories from the past.

Success as an author has become increasingly difficult with the proliferation of **AI generated** copycat books by unscrupulous sellers. They are clever enough to escape copyright action and use dark web tactics to secure paid-for **fake reviews**, something I would never do.

Hence I would like to ask you—I plead with you—the reader, to leave a star rating or review on Amazon. This helps make my book discoverable for new readers, and helps me to compete fairly against the devious copycats.

If this book was a gift to you, you can leave stars or a review on your own Amazon account, or you can ask the gift-giver or a family member to do this on your behalf.

I have enjoyed researching and writing this book for you and would greatly appreciate your feedback.

Best regards,
Bernard Bradforsand-Tyler.

Please leave a
book review/rating at:

https://bit.ly/1967-reviews

Or scan the QR code:

Flashback books make the perfect gift- see the full range at

https://bit.ly/FlashbackSeries

Image Attributions

Photographs and images used in this book are reproduced courtesy of the following:

Page 6 – From *Life* mag, 3rd Feb 1967. Source: books.google.com/books?id=b1YEAAAAMBAJ&printsec (PD image).*
Page 8 – Mamiya C33 advertisement from 1967. Source: flickr.com/photos/nesster/5969799194/ (PD image).*
Page 9 – From *Life* mag, 10th Nov 1967. Source: books.google.com/books?id=51UEAAAAMBAJ&printsec (PD image).*
Page 10 – Poster for the Pow Wow Human Be-In and photo of attendees, 14th January 1967. Creators unknown. Source: digitalstories.famsf.org/summer-of-love/#awakening-in-the-park.**
Page 11 – Harlem protest, source: peacehistory-usfp.org/vietnam-war/. Pre-1978, no mark (PD image). – Veterans protest by Frank Wolfe (White House Office), source: en.wikipedia.org/wiki/March_on_the_Pentagon (PD image).
Page 12 – From *Life* mag, 3rd Feb 1967. Source: books.google.com/books?id=b1YEAAAAMBAJ&printsec (PD image).*
Page 13 – Girls on Carnaby Street, circa 1967. Creator unknown, source: tumblr.com. Pre-1978, no mark (PD).
Page 14 – The Who promotional photo, creator unknown. – Rolling Stones in concert, Sweden, 3rd April 1966 by Ingen Uppgift. Source: commons.wikimedia.org/wiki/File:Kungliga_ Tennishallen_Stones_1966a.jpg. – The Beatles signed photo, source: freeclassicimages.com/images/beatles_autograph.jpg. – Quant dresses,
source: https://en.wikipedia.org/wiki/Miniskirt. All images Pre-1978, no copyright mark (PD image).
Page 15 – Jean Shrimpton, source: search.aol.com/aol/image;_ylt=AwrT4R.VDDZfcdQAiEdjCWVH?q=jean+shrimpton. – Twiggy source: search.aol.com/aol/image;_ylt=Awr9DWs_DzZf1qwAvCtjCWVH?q=twiggy&imgl=fsuc&fr2= p%3As% 2Cv%3Ai. Pre-1978, no copyright mark (PD images). – *Where Eagles Dare* by Alistair MacLean and *The Python Project* by Victor Canning, book dustcovers reproduced in low resolution under fair use terms to illustrate the article only. – *Smashing Time* by Paramount Pictures, and *You Only Live Twice* by Eon Productions and United Artists film posters.**
Page 16 – From *Life* mag, 1st Sept 1967. Source: books.google.com/books?id=UFYEAAAAMBAJ&printsec (PD image).*
Page 17 – Rockers, Mods and ladies group photo. Creators unknown. Pre-1978, no copyright mark (PD image).
Page 18 – From *Life* mag, 7th Apr 1967. Source: books.google.com/books?id=-1UEAAAAMBAJ&printsec (PD image).*
Page 19 – Traffic photos from the '60s, from private unknown sources. Pre-1978, no copyright mark (PD image).
Page 20 – From *Life* mag, 20th Jan 1967. Source: books.google.com/books?id=YIYEAAAAMBAJ&printsec (PD image).*
Page 21 – Chrysler from *Life*, 6th Oct 1967. Source: books.google.com/books?id=2UwEAAAAMBAJ&printsec. – Cadillac from *Life*, 21st Apr 1967. Source: books.google.com/books?id=GFYEAAAAMBAJ&printsec. – Mercury Cougar from *Life*, 19th May 1967. Source: books.google.com.sg/books?id=TVYEAAAAMBAJ&printsec (all images this page PD image)*
Page 22 – 1967 Toyota Corona, source: hemmings.com/stories/article/game-changer-1967-toyota-corona (PD image).* – 1967 Datsun 1300 Sedan, source: flickr.com/photos/aussie-car-adverts/24909067068 (PD image).*
– 1967 Honda N360, source: nurieya.jp/2019/07/27/honda-n360/ (PD image).*
Page 23 – From *Life* mag, 13th Jan 1967. Source: books.google.com/books?id=a1YEAAAAMBAJ&printsec (PD image).*
Page 24 – From *Life* mag, 10th Feb 1967. Source: books.google.com/books?id=eFYEAAAAMBAJ&printsec (PD image).*
Page 25 – Image from Magnavox advertisement, source: imgur.com/gallery/C2E0x (PD image).*
Page 26 – Screen still from *The Lucy Show*, 7th Jan 1963, by Desilu Productions.** Source: commons.wikimedia.org/ wiki/File:Vivian_Vance_Lucille_ Ball_The_Lucy_Show_1963.jpg. – *Gomer Pyle*, U.S.M.C. publicity, 1966, by CBS TV. Source: commons.wikimedia.org/wiki/File:Jim_Nabors_Frank_Sutton_Gomer_Pyle_1966.JPG (PD image). – *Bewitched* publicity, 1964, by Ashmont Productions. Source: ar.m.wikipedia.org/wiki/:ملف‎Bewitched_cast_1964.jpg (PD image).
Page 27 – Carol Burnett charwoman character, 1974.** Source: commons.wikimedia.org/wiki/Category:The_Carol_ Burnett_Show. – *N.Y.P.D.* screen still by ABC.** in 1968, source: commons.wikimedia.org/wiki/Category:N.Y.P.D._ (TV_series). – *Ironside* screen still by NBC.** in 1969, source: commons.wikimedia.org/wiki/Category:Ironside_(TV_ series). – Donahue with Johnny Carson, Aug 1970.** Source: en.wikipedia.org/wiki/Phil_Donahue.
Page 28 – From *Life* mag, 10th Nov 1967. Source: books.google.com/books?id=XkkEAAAAMBAJ&printsec (PD image).*
Page 29 – Chinese Test No. 6. Source: ctbto.org/uploads/pics/China_H-bomb_1967.jpg (PD image). Nevada bomb test, creator unknown. Source: scarc.library.oregonstate.edu/omeka/items/show/1501 (PD image).
Page 30 – Gagarin source: tass.com/society/899827 by Valentin Cheredintsev. – Tereshkova source: cultura.biografie online.it/la-prima-donna-nello-spazio/. – Leonov source: space.com/alexei-leonov-bio.html. All Pre-1978 (PD images).
Page 31 – Apollo 1 crew, photo by NASA. Source: nasa.gov/multimedia/imagegallery/image_feature_2436.html. – Apollo 1 external damage, photo by NASA. Source: commons.wikimedia.org/wiki/Category:Apollo_1_disaster. – Buzz Aldrin on the moon. Source: nasa.gov/mission_pages/apollo/40th/images/apollo_image_12.html. All images this page are PD images.
Page 32 – From *Life* mag, 17th Nov 1967. Source: books.google.com/books?id=bEkEAAAAMBAJ&printsec (PD image).*
Page 33 – From *Life* mag, 3rd Mar 1967. Source: books.google.com/books?id=n1YEAAAAMBAJ&printsec (PD image).*
Page 34 – 9th Marines, South Vietnam 1967, by Defense Dept Photo (Marine Corps) A193030. – U.S.A.F.ground personnel prepare AIM-7E Sparrow missiles for loading on McDonnell F-4C Phantom II aircraft. U.S. Navy photo No. 1996.488.067. 003. Both images source: commons.wikimedia.org/wiki/Category:Vietnam_War_in_1967 (PD images).
Page 35 – War protest photos by US Government photographers Frank Wolfe and S.Sgt. Albert R. Simpson, (Photo identifiers: NARA 530618, ARC 192603 and NAID 594360), 21st Oct 1967. Source: commons.wikimedia.org/wiki/ Category:Demonstrations_and_protests_against_the_Vietnam_War_held_in_the_United_States (PD images).
Page 36 – Images from the WSJ newspaper reproduced here under fair use terms. The images are relevant to the article created and are too small to be used to make illegal copies for use in another book. It is believed the images do not devalue the ability of the copyright holders to profit from the original works in any way.
Page 37 – Detroit riots, creator unknown. Source: blac.media/news-features/a-look-back-at-civil-rights-history/. Pre-1978, no copyright mark (PD image). – New York protest by Al Ravenna, 1967. Photo is from the Library of Congress, World Telegram & Sun photo collection, LOC control 97502365 Reproduction Number: LC-USZ62-117554 (PD image).*
Page 38 – From *Life* mag, 13th Oct 1967. Source: books.google.com/books?id=OUkEAAAAMBAJ&printsec (PD image).*

Page 39 – *National Geographic*, Nov 1967. Source: flickr.com/photos/91591049@N00/15287221545/ (PD image).*
Page 40 – Photos by Li Zhensheng courtesy of Contact Press Images. Images where not in the public domain are here under fair use terms. They are relevant to the article created and too small to be used to make illegal copies. It is believed the images do not devalue the ability of the copyright holders to profit from the original works in any way.
Page 41 – From the National Photo Collection of Israel, digital ID: D327-036. Source: commons.wikimedia.org/wiki/Category:Six-Day_War_in_the_Golan_Heights and commons.wikimedia.org/wiki/ Category:Jerusalem_in_the_1967_Arab-Israeli_War. Pre-1978, no copyright mark (PD images).
Page 42 – From *Life* mag, 6th Jan 1967. Source: books.google.com/books?id=i1YEAAAAMBAJ&printsec (PD image).*
Page 43 – From *Life* mag, 14th Apr 1967. Source: books.google.com/books?id=H1YEAAAAMBAJ&printsec (PD image).*
Page 44 – Promo photo from *Bonnie and Clyde* by Warner Bros. Source: commons.wikimedia.org/wiki/Category: Faye_ Dunaway, (PD image). – Screen still from *Guess Who's Coming to Dinner* by Columbia Pictures.** Courtesy Everett Collection. – Hoffman in 1968. Source: en.wikipedia.org/wiki/Dustin_Hoffman, (PD image).
Page 45 – *The Graduate* movie poster, 1967, by United Artists.** Source: en.wikipedia.org/wiki/The_Graduate. – *To Sir With Love* movie poster, 1967, by Columbia Pictures.** Source: en.wikipedia.org/wiki/To_Sir,_with_Love. – *Valley of the Dolls* movie poster, 1967, by 20th Century Fox.** Source: en.wikipedia.org/wiki/Valley_of_the_Dolls_(film).
Page 46 – Cropped still from *The Good, The Bad and The Ugly* by Produzioni Europee Associati / United Artists.** – Bridgitte Bardot, source: flickr.com/photos/classicvintage/9274563680. Attribution-(CC BY 4.0). – Sophia Loren, source: commons.wikimedia.org/wiki/Category:Sophia_Loren_in_1962. Pre-1978, no mark (PD image).
Page 47 – *You Only Die Twice* movie poster, 1967, by United Artisits.** – *The Karate Killers* movie poster, 1967, by MGM.** – *The Double Man* movie poster, 1967, by Warner Bros.** – *The Deadly Affair* movie poster, 1967, by Columbia Pictures.**
Page 48 – From *Life* mag, 7th Apr 1967. Source: books.google.com/books?id=-1UEAAAAMBAJ&printsec (PD image).*
Page 49 – The Beachboys 1967 press photo by Capitol Records. Source: commons.wikimedia.org/wiki/Category: Group_photographs_of_the_Beach_Boys#/media/File:Beach_Boys_1967.jpg. – The Tempations promotional photo by Mowtown Records. Source: commons.wikimedia.org/wiki/Category:The_Temptations#/media/File:The_Temptations_1968.JPG. All images this page Pre-1978, no copyright mark (PD images).
Page 50 – Poster for the *Monterey Pop Festival* by Tom Wilkes, 1967.** Source: en.wikipedia.org/wiki/Monterey_Pop_Festival#/media/File:Monterey_International_Pop_Music_Festival_poster.jpg. – Janis Joplin, 18th April 1969 in New York City by Elliot Landy, source: commons.wikimedia.org/wiki/File:Janis_Joplin_in_1969.png, Attribution-Share Alike 4.0 International. – Jimi Hendrix 24th May 1967, Stockholm, Sweden. Source: commons.wikimedia.org/wiki/File: Jimi_Hendrix_1967uncropped.jpg. Pre-1978, no copyright mark (PD image).
Page 51 – Jefferson Airplane at *Fantasy Fair and Magic Mountain Music Festival*, 1967. Source: en.wikipedia.org/wiki/Fantasy_Fair_and_Magic_Mountain_Music_Festival#/. – The Doors promotional photo by Elektra Records-Joel Brodsky. Source: commons.wikimedia.org/wiki/Category:The_Doors#/. – Cast of *Hair*, Finland. Source: commons.wikimedia.org/wiki/Category:Hair_(musical). All images this page pre-1978, no copyright mark (PD images).
Page 52 – From *Life* mag, 20th Jan 1967. Source: books.google.com/books?id=YlYEAAAAMBAJ&printsec (PD* image).
Page 53 – Posters from USA Library of Congress. Control Numbers: 95504681, 92517368 & 2014647489 (PD images).
Page 54 – The Supremes publicity photo by General Artists Corporation from 22nd Dec 1967. Source: commons. wikimedia.org/ wiki/Category:The_Supremes#/media/File:The_Supremes_1967.JPG. – Frank and Nancy Sinatra for CBS Television in 1966, source: commons.wikimedia.org/wiki/Category:Nancy_Sinatra#/media/File:Frank_and_Nancy_Sinatra_ 1966.jpg. – Lulu on the set of Fanclub, 1965, Dutch TV. Source: en.wikipedia.org/wiki/Lulu_%28singer%29. – The Monkees publicity photo, 15th Sep 1966, for NBC Television. Source: commons.wikimedia.org/wiki/Category: The_Monkees#/media/File:The_ Monkees_1966.JPG. All images this page Pre-1978, no copyright mark (PD images).
Page 55 – Aretha Franklin publicity by Atlantic Records from Billboard, 17th Feb 1968. Source: commons.wikimedia. org/wiki/Category:Aretha_Franklin. Pre-1978 (PD image). – Stevie Wonder, 30th July 1967, by Nijs, Jac. de/ Anefo for Nationaal Archief, CC0. Source: commons.wikimedia.org/wiki/Category:Stevie_Wonder_in_1967 (PD image).
Page 56 – Source: Montgomery Ward catalog, Summer 1967 (PD image).*
Page 57 – Models in office attire and tea dresses, early '50s. Creators unknown. Pre-1978, no copyright mark (PD image). – Jacqueline Kennedy on the steps of the Elysee Palace, France, 31st May 1961. From the JFK Library. Source: commons.wikimedia.org/wiki/File:President_De_Gaulle_stands_between_President_Kennedy_and_Mrs._Kennedy_on_the_steps_of_the_Elysee_Palace.jpg (PD image). – Jacqueline Kennedy in India, 1962. Source: flickr.com/photos/usembassynewdelhi/6914524677 by U.S. Embassy New Delhi. Attribution-(CC BY-ND 4.0). – Jacqueline Kennedy at the White House 11th May '62. Source:zh.m.wikipedia.org/wiki/File:JBKJFKMalraux.jpg. US Government photo (PD image).
Page 58 – Mod fashions, source: vintag.es/2016/07/mod-fashion-characteristic-of-british.html. Pre-1978, (PD images).
Page 59 – Models wearing Mary Quant mini dresses, creator unknown. Source: thedabbler.co.uk/2012/10/granny-takes-a-trip-back-in-time/. Pre-1978, no copyright mark (PD image). – London street scene, creator unknown. Source: vintag.es/2016/07/mod-fashion-characteristic-of-british.html. Pre-1978, no copyright mark (PD image). – Mary Quant, 16th Dec 1966. Source: commons.wikimedia.org/wiki/File:Mary_Quant_in_a_minidress_(1966).jpg by Jac. de Nijs / Anefo from the Dutch National Archives. License: Creative Commons Attribution-Share Alike 3.0 Netherlands.
– Models wearing Mary Quant plastic raincoats and boots, creator unknown. Pre-1978, no copyright mark (PD image).
Page 60 – Penelope Tree, photographer Richard Avedon for *Vogue* Oct 1967. – Jean Shrimpton for *Vogue* September 1967, Twiggy for *Italian Vogue*, July 1967, and various photo of Twiggy, dates, photographers, source unknown.
Images reproduced this page under terms of Fair Use are used sparingly for information only, are significant to the article created and are rendered in low resolution to avoid piracy. It is believed that these images will not in any way limit the ability of the copyright owners to sell their product.

Page 61 – From *Life* mag, 2nd Jun 1967. Source: books.google.com/books?id=fFYEAAAAMBAJ&printsec (PD image).*
Page 62 – André Courrèges fur trimmed hat, creator unknown, source: alchetron.com/André-Courrèges. – Striped suits and slit glasses, creator unknown, source: vivavintageclothing.com/blog/a-salute-to-space-age-1960s-designer-andres-courreges/. – Cutout dress, photographed by William Laxton. Source: artlyst.com/news/andre-courreges-french-fashion-designer-painter-and-sculptor-dies-at-92/. – Space Bride by Jezebel, NY 1966. Images this page may be copyrighted by the creator. They are reproduced under fair use terms and rendered in low resolution to avoid piracy. It is believed these images will not in any way limit the ability of the copyright owner to market or sell their product.
Page 63 – Models wearing fashions from the late '60s. Photographers unknown. Pre-1978, (PD images). – The Beatles. Source: commons.wikimedia.org/wiki/File:The_Beatles_magical_mystery_tour_(cropped).jpg. Attribution-(CC BY 3.0).
Page 64 – From *Life* mag, 2nd Jun 1967. Source: books.google.com/books?id=fFYEAAAAMBAJ&printsec (PD image).*
Page 65 – Expo 67, Saint-Helen Island, pavilions of Switzerland, Austria and Iran; thematic pavilion Man the Explorer. Montréal, Québec, Canada. Source: commons.wikimedia.org/wiki/Category:Pavilions_of_Expo_1967. Attribution-(CC BY-SA 3.0). – Lawrence, circa 1967. Source: commons.wikimedia.org/wiki/Category:Robert_Henry_Lawrence,_Jr. (PD image). – Bell, 15th June 1967. Source: commons.wikimedia.org/wiki/Category: Jocelyn_Bell_Burnell. Attribution-(CC BY-SA 2.0).
Page 66 – From *Life* mag, 6th Oct 1967. Source: books.google.com/books?id=2UwEAAAAMBAJ&printsec (PD image).*
Page 67 – Switzer, Boston 19th Apr 1967. Source: commons.wikimedia.org/wiki/Category:Kathrine_Switzer. Attribution (CC BY-SA 2.0). – Ali, circa 1966. Source: commons.wikimedia.org/wiki/Category:Muhammad_Ali (PD image).
Page 68 & 69 – Ronald and Nancy Reagan, creator unknown, 1964. Source: commons.wikimedia.org/wiki/Ronald_Reagan (PD image). – Brooke at the Republican National Convention, 1968. Creator: Thomas J. O'Halloran, 6th Aug 1968. From the Library of Congress, Reproduction Number: LC-DIG-ds-08052 (PD image). – Suharto, official portrait 1978 (PD image). – One Hundred Years of Solitude book cover original edition from 1967. – Marshall, 1967, by Yoichi R. Okamoto. From the National Archives and Records Administration, NAID: 2803441. – Guevara, 1960, by Alberto Korda. From the Museo Che Guevara, Havana Cuba.– Holt, 1966, by Ronald Hall. From US Department of Defence, source: commons.wikimedia.org/wiki/Category:Harold_Holt. All images this page are in the Public Domain.
Page 70 – Canada Dry print magazine advertisement, 1967. Source: eBay
Page 71 – Delta Airlines print magazine advertisement, 1967. Source: eBay

Page 72-74 – All photos are, where possible, CC BY 2.0 or PD images made available by the creator for free use including commercial use. Where commercial use photos are unavailable, photos are included here for information only under U.S. fair use laws due to: 1- images are low resolution copies; 2- images do not devalue the ability of the copyright holders to profit from the original works in any way; 3- Images are too small to be used to make illegal copies for use in another book; 4- The images are relevant to the article created.
Page 75 – From *Life* mag, 13th Jan 1967. Source: books.google.com/books?id=a1YEAAAAMBAJ&printsec (PD image).*
Page 78 – Goodyear Tires print magazine advertisement, 1967. Source: eBay
Page 79 – Honda print magazine advertisement, 1967. Source: eBay

*Advertisement (or image from an advertisement) is in the public domain because it was published in a collective work (such as a periodical issue) in the US between 1925 and 1977 and without a copyright notice specific to the advertisement.
**Posters for movies or events are either in the public domain (published in the US between 1925 and 1977 and without a copyright notice specific to the artwork) or owned by the production company, creator, or distributor of the movie or event. Posters, where not in the public domain, and screen stills from movies or TV shows, are reproduced here under USA Fair Use laws due to: 1- images are low resolution copies; 2- images do not devalue the ability of the copyright holders to profit from the original works in any way; 3- Images are too small to be used to make illegal copies for use in another book; 4- The images are relevant to the article created.

This book was written by Bernard Bradforsand-Tyler as part of *A Time Traveler's Guide* series of books.

All rights reserved. The author exerts the moral right to be identified as the author of the work.

No parts of this book may be reproduced, stored in any retrieval system, or transmitted in any form or by any means, without prior written permission from the author.

This is a work of nonfiction. No names have been changed, no events have been fabricated. The content of this book is provided as a source of information for the reader, however it is not meant as a substitute for direct expert opinion. Although the author has made every effort to ensure that the information in this book is correct at time of printing, and while this publication is designed to provide accurate information in regard to the subject matters covered, the author assumes no responsibility for errors, inaccuracies, omissions, or any other inconsistencies herein and hereby disclaims any liability to any party for any loss, damage, or disruption caused by errors or omissions.

All images contained herein are reproduced with the following permissions:
- Images included in the public domain.
- Images obtained under creative commons license.
- Images included under fair use terms.
- Images reproduced with owner's permission.

All image attributions and source credits are provided at the back of the book. All images are the property of their respective owners and are protected under international copyright laws.

First printed in 2022 in the USA (ISBN 978-1-922676-04-7) and 2024 (ISBN 978-1-922676-15-3).
Revised in 2024, 2nd Edition (ISBN 978-1-922676-17-7).
Self-published by B. Bradforsand-Tyler.

www.ingramcontent.com/pod-product-compliance
Lightning Source LLC
Chambersburg PA
CBHW072104110526
44590CB00018B/3315